Readings in
Business Logistics

AMA Reprint Series
Editor John J. Wheatley

Engel (ed.)   *Consumer Behavior: Selected Readings*

McConaughy (ed.)   *Readings in Business Logistics*

Rathmell (ed.)   *Salesmanship: Selected Readings*

Wheatley (ed.)   *Measuring Advertising Effectiveness: Selected Readings*

Readings in
Business Logistics

Edited for the
AMERICAN MARKETING ASSOCIATION
by
DAVID McCONAUGHY, Ph.D.
Assistant Professor of Marketing
University of Southern California

AMA Reprint Series
1969

Richard D. Irwin, Inc., Homewood, Illinois
Irwin-Dorsey Limited, Georgetown, Ontario

First Printing, January, 1969

Library of Congress Catalog Card No. 69–15542

Printed in the United States of America

Preface

Business logistics is the process inherent in a distribution system that moves materials and products from their producer to their consumer. Such a system, viewed in a comprehensive manner, includes a significant portion of the activity which takes place in the channel of distribution, especially that concerned with transportation and storage, the physical product flow, and the inventory maintained in the channel.

The definition and concepts of business logistics systems have evolved over many years, with recent emphasis somewhat divided into the study of (1) distribution channels and middlemen, and (2) physical distribution processes. These approaches do not represent a divided opinion with respect to distribution, but are a study of different dimensions of the subject.

By design, the scope of this collection of articles is focused primarily on the logistics process. The articles presented are grouped under the headings of Introduction to Business Logistics, Logistics Systems Analysis, Logistics of Distribution Channels, and Management of Business Logistics. The major sections thus designated, articles of significance appearing within the past ten years in AMA publications have been selected for inclusion in each of them.

These readings, then, provide a single source of recent AMA-sponsored contributions to the field of business logistics. The resulting volume is an anthology of material in logistics that could be used as a convenient supplementary readings book for introductory courses in marketing, marketing management, and channels of distribution; or as a bookshelf type of reference.

In the conception and preparation of this volume I wish to acknowledge the helpful comments and suggestions of John Wheatley and Taylor Meloan.

December, 1968   DAVID MCCONAUGHY

v

Table of contents

Part IV. Management of business logistics

Introduction

This short book is one of a new series being published by the American Marketing Association. It is designed to make available in a convenient form the latest scholarly research and writing on a series of topics which are of continuing interest to practitioners, students, and teachers in the field of marketing. It is our hope that this format will be successful in bringing such material to the attention of persons who are not members of the Association as well as of those who are members of the AMA but who have not had the opportunity to read, in their original sources, the articles that have been included in this volume. Many of the publications that have been drawn upon in connection with this endeavor have had a relatively limited circulation in spite of the fact that they contain a substantial number of significant contributions to the literature dealing with various aspects of business logistics.

JOHN J. WHEATLEY
General Editor

Part I

INTRODUCTION TO BUSINESS LOGISTICS

The articles in this section focus on the description of business logistics concepts and principal problem areas. Objectives of logistics systems and means of achieving these objectives are explored, and a perspective on logistics and physical distribution is presented.

Hill (1) in "Distribution Systems Management: Keys to Profit in the Sixties" presents five main profit-related decisions commonly faced in logistics management. He illustrates these key decisions with a series of hypothetical examples which give substance to his discussion of logistics decision making. Nelson (2) in "Distribution Ideas in a Changing Market" proposes a periodic distribution audit so that a firm continually adapts its logistics system to changing markets. Heskett (3) in "Spatial and Temporal Aspects of Physical Distribution" presents an excellent summary of writings on spatial location and time dimensions of physical distribution and proposes desirable attributes of distribution models. Smykay (4) discusses "The Role of Physical Distribution in Marketing Organization." Parker (5) in "Improved Efficiency and Reduced Cost in Marketing" examines factors which have shown promise in reducing the cost of physical distribution. He outlines several instances where a substitution of air freight for field warehousing or storage has improved customer service at a lower total cost. Banks (6) in "The Relationship of Transportation to Distribution" discusses the logistics and physical distribution system implications of transportation services. He cautions against measuring logistics tasks by ton-mile and freight rate criteria, and suggests a total service and cost approach. Concluding this section, Schneider (7) in "Milestones on the Road of Physical Distribution" examines changes that have taken place in the characteristics and management of logistics problems. New techniques of analysis and the availability of automatic data processing systems are shown to have markedly changed the physical distribution task. The result has been a change in organization for physical distribution in many firms and a change in college logistics courses and research activities.

1. DISTRIBUTION SYSTEMS MANAGEMENT: KEY TO PROFITS IN THE SIXTIES*

W. Clayton Hill

"Fifty cents of each dollar for distribution is too high," says the Department of Commerce; "exorbitant," exclaims the consumer; "cannot live with this," cries the businessman. Fifty cents for distribution may be an exaggerated figure, but distribution is certainly one of the major costs of doing business, loaded with opportunities and challenges for marketing people. Manufacturing people long ago recognized the necessity for constant system improvement and cost reduction, with the result that manufacturing costs have been reduced to a level that unit savings now are figured in terms of mills and pennies. But opportunities for unit savings in distribution run not in terms of mills and pennies, but in terms of nickels, dimes, and dollars.

Surely, then, the *"Key to Profits in the Sixties"* for most companies will be in distribution systems management—distribution cost reduction and, more particularly, the improvement of service to consumers. Consumers today, with their many needs fulfilled, will buy only from those who can deliver the goods when and where they are wanted. If one then can visualize the flow of goods from factory to consumers as a distribution pipeline, he can quickly frame a picture of the opportunities in distribution. For in the flow of goods from the factory to the consumer, whenever the product stops in its movement, costs add up and service deteriorates. When the products are moving in a continuous flow, distribution service is maximized and cost minimized.

OBJECTIVES OF DISTRIBUTION SYSTEMS MANAGEMENT

The objectives of distribution systems management are simple—three in number—but in opposition to each other.

First, maximize service—both order and delivery service.

Second, minimize distribution costs—transportation, inventory maintenance, warehousing, data processing, all those costs essential and necessary in initiating, controlling and effecting flow of goods to the customer.

Third, maximize information feedback—distribution information feedback to marketing headquarters, and manufacturing, so that products can be kept moving in as near a continuous flow as possible and so that

*From *Marketing Precision and Executive Action*, American Marketing Association, Summer, 1962, pp. 121–38.

guidelines are furnished to the manufacturing organization for production scheduling.

We have, then, three major objectives that are conflicting in nature. How can one maximize service and at the same time reduce costs? How can one reduce costs and at the same time provide maximum information feedback to the factory? The real answer is to optimize service and costs to arrive at the best balance of these factors for profitable progress of the business.

FIVE KEY PROFIT DECISIONS

In this challenging task of optimizing service and cost in distribution systems management, five key profit decisions must be made.

Decision 1: Number of distribution points. What is the optimum number of distribution points for national distribution in the United States today? In the environment of the sixties a company distribution on a nationwide basis can do an effective job with 25 or less distribution points.

Decision 2: Customer service level. In discussing what kind of service is provided to the customer, measurements have too long been missing. Customer service level *can* be quantified, such as a 90 percent customer service level, meaning that 90 percent of a customer's order to a distribution point would be delivered on the average within one day. Customer service level decisions have a major impact on service and profits.

Decision 3: Warehouse replenishment time. The rapidity with which an item sold from a warehouse can be replaced from the factory has a marked effect upon the amount of inventory that must be carried. A more rapid system response reduces costs.

Decision 4: Selective stocking. Is it really necessary to stock every single item in every distribution point? Or does the proper balance of service and cost call for the stocking of the fast-moving items in each distribution point with the slow-moving items backed up at a limited number of control points?

Decision 5: Total system optimization. And finally, total distribution systems optimization—number of distribution points, customer service level, warehouse replenishment time, and selective stocking—balancing service and cost is *the key to profits in the sixties.*

HYPO COMPANY

Developing the opportunities in distribution systems management can probably be done more clearly and simply by using an example, "The Hypo Company." Although we will use Hypo for illustration, the data was assimilated from an intensive study of some 65 distribution points of varying sizes handling a wide variety of products. Hypo is a fairly typical company with annual sales volume of $50,000,000, shipping 500,000 units at an average price of $100 each. The product has a value of $1 per pound. The company produces and sells 1,000 stock items and has 10,000 dealers to serve through a 100-point distribution system. The factory is located at Indianapolis, Indiana. Warehouse replenishment time is 25 days. With this background we will review our five key decision areas and their effect on "Hypo."

DECISION 1: NUMBER OF DISTRIBUTION POINTS

Hypo has a 100-point distribution system, but let us compare alternative systems of 5, 17, 25 and 50 points as illustrated in Figure 1.

FIGURE 1

DECISION 1. NUMBER OF DISTRIBUTION POINTS
SERVICE/COST COMPARISON;
FIVE ALTERNATIVE SYSTEMS; LOGISTICS ONLY

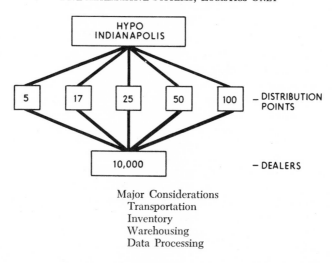

Major Considerations
Transportation
Inventory
Warehousing
Data Processing

What are the major considerations in determining the proper number of distribution points? They are first, the cost of transportation both from the Hypo factory to the distribution points and from the distribution points to the dealers; second, the inventory investment in the distribution pipeline; third, the cost of operating and maintaining the warehouses; and fourth, the cost of data processing. All four factors must be evaluated individually from a service/cost viewpoint and then optimized in total.

Transportation. Transportation has experienced revolutionary changes in the past 25 years. Have we, as marketers, recognized them? In the 1930's trucks were 20 to 25 feet long and averaged about 25 miles per hour on the road; today, trucks are 40 to 45 feet long and can average 50 miles per hour on our turnpikes, e.g., 16 hours from Chicago to New York. In only the last 10 years turnpikes from New York to Chicago, Buffalo, Boston, and Washington have been opened. Other parts of the country are building superhighways with great speed. Soon, there will be a nationwide system. Airfreight in the past five years has carried increasing tonnages of freight. In the railroad industry, piggyback, Flexivan, drop-off services, etc., have been added in the last five to six years. The transportation system of the United States today is as different as today's automated production lines are from those of 15 years ago. Yet I am afraid marketers have not fully exploited the opportunities in these changes. With today's transportation systems and changes, 90 percent of the U.S. market can be delivered in one day with 25 distribution points. Table 1 compares transportation service and cost under our five alternative distribution systems.

With 100 distribution points, 99 percent of the U.S. market can be delivered in one day, the remainder the second day, at an annual cost of $1,847,000. With 25 points, 90 percent of the U.S. market can be delivered in one day, the remainder the second day, at an annual cost of $2,082,000—10 percent to 20 percent more than the 100-point system. Even with 5 points, 33 percent of the U.S. market can be delivered in one day, 53 percent the second day, the remainder the third day, at an annual cost of $2,632,000—35 percent to 45 percent more than the 100-point system.

Transportation costs are predicated on CL (carload) rates from the Indianapolis factory to the distribution points and LTL (less than truckload) and metropolitan rates from the distribution points to the customers.

We may then conclude from a transportation viewpoint that more distribution points provide better service and at less cost. But transportation is not the only factor in the logistics of distribution.

TABLE 1

DECISION 1. NUMBER OF DISTRIBUTION POINTS
TRANSPORTATION—SERVICE/COST

	Delivery Service		Transportation Costs	
Number of Distribution Points	% U.S. Market Delivered 1st Day	% U.S. Market Delivered 2 Days	Annual Costs (in Thousands)	Cost Index
100	99	1	$1,847	100%
50	96	4	1,934	105–100%
25	90	10	2,082	110–120
17	81	16	2,211	120–130
5	33	53	2,632	135–145

CL Rate—Indianapolis to Distribution Point

LTL and Metro Rates—Distribution Point to Customer

More Points—Better Service
More Points—Less Cost

Inventory. How does the investment in inventories and the cost of maintaining these inventories stack up? Table 2 presents this picture.

TABLE 2

DECISION 1. NUMBER OF DISTRIBUTION POINTS
INVENTORY INVESTMENT/MAINTENANCE COSTS

	Investment			Maintenance Costs	
Number of Distribution Points	Hypo Inventory (in Thousands)	Inventory Investment Index		Hypo Cost @ 22% (in Thousands)	Inventory Maintenance Cost Index
100	$14,418	100%		$3,172	100%
50	11,423	75–85		2,513	75–85
25	9,079	60–70		1,997	60–70
17	8,004	50–60		1,761	50–60
5	5,475	35–45		1,205	35–45

25 Days Replenishment Time	Capital Charges,
90% Customer Service Level	Insurance, Taxes,
	Depreciation and Obsolescence,
	Storage and Space....22%

More Points—More Inventory—Greater Maintenance Costs

Hypo's 100-point distribution system for its $50,000,000 business—90 percent customer service level and 25-day replenishment time—requires $14,418,000 in inventory at an annual maintenance cost of $3,172,000. The 25-point system calls for $9,079,000 in inventory and $1,997,000 in maintenance costs—60 to 70 percent of the 100-point system. The 5-point system carries $5,475,000 in inventory, $1,205,000 in maintenance costs, 35 to 45 percent of the 100-point system. The cost factor for inventory maintenance is 22 percent of inventory, made up of capital charges, insurance, taxes, depreciation, obsolescence, storage, and space costs.

To sum up, more points require more inventory and greater maintenance costs.

Warehouse handling costs. Our third consideration in optimizing the number of distribution points is warehouse handling costs. These are the costs of physically moving merchandise into the warehouse, locating, retrieving and loading for outgoing delivery, and are portrayed in Table 3.

Hypo's 100-point system costs $514,000 a year for warehouse handling, but a 25-point system would cost $265,000 a year, or 45 to 55 percent of the 100-point system. A 5-point system would cost $190,000 a year, or 35 to 45 percent of the 100-point system.

Our conclusion, then, is that the more points in the distribution system, the greater the costs of warehouse handling.

Data processing costs. Data processing, our fourth major area of consideration, includes such elements as order service, inventory con-

TABLE 3

DECISION 1. NUMBER OF DISTRIBUTION POINTS
WAREHOUSE HANDLING COSTS
(present methods)

Number of Distribution Points	Hypo Cost (in Thousands)	Warehousing Cost Index
100	$514	100%
50	368	65–75
25	265	45–55
17	235	40–50
5	190	35–45

Receiving—Retrieving
Locating—Loading

More Points—Greater Warehouse Costs

trol, billing, accounting and other paperwork necessary in effectively operating a distribution system. Table 4 summarizes these costs, using manual methods. Were computers and wire communications used the results would be more favorable for a smaller number of distribution points.

TABLE 4

DECISION 1. NUMBER OF DISTRIBUTION POINTS
DATA PROCESSING COSTS
(present methods)

Number of Distribution Points	Hypo Costs (in Thousands)	Data Processing Cost Index
100	$777	100%
50	585	70–80
25	496	60–70
17	486	60–70
5	448	55–65

Order Service
Inventory Control
Billing

More Points—Greater Data Processing Costs

Hypo's 100-point system data processing costs are $777,000 a year. With a 25-point system, the costs are $496,000 annually, 60 to 70 percent of the 100-point system. A 5-point system cost would be $448,000 a year, or 55 to 65 percent of the 100-point system.

The more points, the greater the data processing costs.

Optimizing number of distribution points. Now that we have evalu-

FIGURE 2

DECISION 1. NUMBER OF DISTRIBUTION POINTS
HYPO

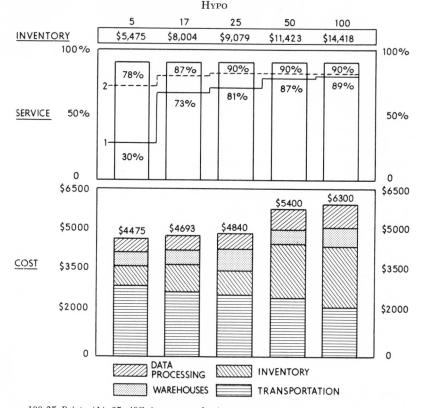

100-25 Points (1) 35–40% inventory reduction.
          (2) 9% reduction 1st day service *only*.
          (3) 20-25% cost reduction.

ated each factor individually from a service/cost viewpoint, Figure 2 illustrates total optimization for the number of distribution points.

First, with Hypo's present 100-point system, 90 percent of the customers in the United States can be delivered in one day, with the remainder in the second day. But the associated costs for transportation, inventory maintenance, warehousing, and data processing are $6,300,000 annually.

With a 25-point system 81 percent of the customers' orders could be delivered in the first day, 90 percent in two days, and the remainder in the third day. This 25-point system would cost $4,840,000 annually for transportation, inventory maintenance, warehouse handling, and data processing. And with the 5-point system, 30 percent of the customers' orders could be delivered the first day, 78 percent in the first and second days, and all customers' orders by the third day, at a cost of $4,475,000 annually. If Hypo reduced its distribution system from 100 to 25 points, major results would accrue. Inventories would be reduced 35 to 40 percent. First-day delivery service only would suffer by 9 percent but the cost reductions would be nearly $1,500,000, or 20 to 25 percent.

Hypo management after careful consideration decided to use a 25-point system. They reasoned that a $1,500,000 savings represented 3 percent on sales and that new approaches to customer service levels would more than compensate for the 9 percent reduction in first-day delivery service.

DECISION 2: CUSTOMER SERVICE LEVEL

Here is an area that has long needed measuring and quantifying. Today, computers have made this possible. What do we mean by customer service level? It may be defined as the percentage of products available for shipment to customers on the day an order is received. Many marketing people will vigorously insist that customer service level must be 100 percent, not realizing the economics involved nor knowing their present service level. In one such analysis it was found that one and one-fourth years total production would be required in inventory to give a 99 percent service level, and with further analysis the actual customer service level was less than 70 percent. Now with a method of measurement, rational economic analyses and decisions can be made. It is significant to note that a customer service level designation means a balanced inventory, e.g., a 90 percent C.S.L. (customer service level) refers to each individual product in the inventory.

Figure 3 shows the effect on inventories of various service levels at Hypo's Boston warehouse.

These service levels are predicated on a 25-day warehouse replenishment time. A 75 percent C.S.L. at Hypo's Boston warehouse requires

FIGURE 3

DECISION 2. CUSTOMER SERVICE LEVEL
HYPO: BOSTON WAREHOUSE CUSTOMER SERVICE LEVEL

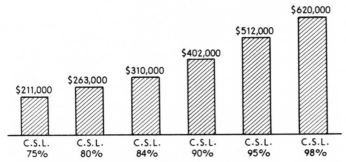

Policy Decision—Affects Customer Strategy

Note: 25-Day replenishment time

a $211,000 inventory; a 90 percent C.S.L., $402,000 inventory, almost twice as much. And a 98 percent C.S.L. requires $620,000 in inventory, almost three times the 75 percent service level. Hypo management chose a 90 percent C.S.L., since this would be a 20 percent improvement over their present operations.

The decision establishing the customer service level for a business is a policy decision, one that has important effects on the strategy of the business. This decision is as important to the business as a decision with respect to return on investment for building a new plant or for bringing out a new product.

Then, too, customer service level provides another tool for the business to use in competition in addition to price, technical service, etc. A business could provide a 95 percent C.S.L. in a new market until it becomes well established or for competitive reasons, and then shifting to a 90 percent or 85 percent or 80 percent level as conditions change.

DECISION 3: WAREHOUSE REPLENISHMENT TIME

What do we mean by warehouse replenishment time? This is the time required for the distribution system to replace a unit sold by the distribution point. It includes the time required for information that a unit has been sold to get to the factory, factory processing, transportation of the merchandise to the distribution point and into its inventory ready for sale. Warehouse replenishment time has substantial effect upon the cost of operating the distribution system, as shown in Table 5.

Three major factors make up warehouse replenishment time. First, the order frequency, or how often the distribution point totals up its orders and sends the information back to the factory; next, the time required for the orders to get back to the factory; and, after the orders are received at the factory, the time required to process the order and

TABLE 5

DECISION 3. WAREHOUSE REPLENISHMENT TIME
HYPO: EFFECT OF REPLENISHMENT TIME REDUCTION
BOSTON WAREHOUSE INVENTORY

	Replenishment Time (Days)	
Order frequency	14	1
Communications	3	1
Factory processing, transit	8	8
Total	25	10

	Units	Amount
25-Day lead time	4,020	$402,000
10-Day lead time	2,080	208,000
Net reduction	1,940	$194,000

Internal Procedure Decision—No Customer Effect

transport the merchandise back to the distribution point. Table 5 illustrates the difference between a 25-day and a 10-day warehouse replenishment time at Hypo's Boston warehouse. The 25-day replenishment time is predicated on an order frequency of 14 days, which is fairly normal. This means that the distribution point goes through its stock cards or other records at least every two weeks, totals up what is needed and sends the order into the factory. The order is sent in by mail, which, on the average, takes three more days. Factory, processing, and transit time back to the distribution point take 8 days, a total of 25 days. With the 25-day replenishment time 4,020 units and $402,000 of inventory is required at Hypo's Boston warehouse.

Now, let us speed up the replenishment time. Instead of waiting two weeks to add up the cards and order, let us send a daily report to the factory of the units sold each day. And, instead of mailing the report, let us use teletype, which means the factory will have the information the next morning. Still maintaining our factory processing and transit time at 8 days, we now have a total of 10 days replenishment time. With this 10-day replenishment time only 2,080 units, or $208,000 of inventory, is needed, an inventory reduction of $194,000, almost 50 percent. Hypo management decided to reduce their warehouse replenishment time from 25 to 10 days.

The warehouse replenishment time decision is an internal one, involving procedure changes only. It can be made merely by designing the procedures and putting them into effect, with no effect upon the customer. Some costs will be added—teletype, daily processing—but the savings and improved service far outweigh these costs.

DECISION 4: SELECTIVE STOCKING

The fourth decision area—selective stocking—offers major opportunities for cost savings in the logistics of distribution. Our manufacturing friends long ago classified their inventories into A, B, C classifications, etc., the A items being those that move rapidly, the B items moving less rapidly, and the C items with even a slower rate of turnover.

Figure 4 shows a similar classification system for finished goods and the implications.

This data prepared from some 65 distribution points and a great variety of products shows that the A items—the top 5 percent of the products—produce 72 percent of the sales and require 44 percent of the inventory. The B items—the next 10 percent of the products—produce 16 percent of the sales but require 23 percent of the inventory. The C items—the next 15 percent of the products—produce 8 percent of the sales and require 17 percent of the inventory. And the D items—the remaining 70 percent of the products—produce only 4 percent of the sales with 16 percent of the inventory.

These distributions seem to follow some fairly general economic laws that present themselves in any mass of data with respect to people and

FIGURE 4

Decision 4. Selective Stocking
Hypo: Breakdown of Sales By Item
Typical Business and Boston Warehouse

A items—small inventory.
B, C and D items—large inventory.

sales. It has been shown in many situations, such as population, students' grades, customers' purchases, product sales, etc., that about 20 percent of the items will account for 80 percent of activity, and 80 percent of the items will account for about 20 percent of activity. Selective stocking is a dramatic opportunity for management to accomplish important savings, as shown for Hypo in Table 6.

In the Hypo Boston warehouse, stocking A and B items in Boston and C and D items at the factory will reduce costs $19,071 per year; service on A and B would be the same, C and D items less favorable.

TABLE 6

Selective Stocking Alternative
Hypo: Boston Warehouse
(A and B items at Boston; C and D items, stocking alternatives)

	(1) At Factory Using LTL	(2) At Factory Using Air Freight	(3) At New York Using LTL
Inventory at Boston Reduction in inventory	$112,540	$112,540	$112,540
Cost			
Net cost reduction	$ 19,071	$ 2,311	$ 15,116
Delivery service (days)			
A and B items (88% total sales)			
90% C.S.L.	Same	Same	Same
C and D items (12% total sales)			
90% C.S.L.	6–7	4–5	3–4

C and D, Factory—LTL—Lowest Cost
C and D, New York—LTL—Best Service

These savings accrue even though additional costs are incurred in using teletype communication and LTL freight for speeding factory service on C and D items. Using air freight from the factory on C and D items results in a saving of $2,311 per year, with service on C and D items 4 to 5 days. But stocking the A and B items at Boston with the C and D items in a regional warehouse in New York, serving the eastern seaboard, gives a cost reduction of $15,116 a year, same service on A and B items and three- to four-day service on C and D items. Hypo management chose this regional back-up plan.

Hypo system—customer service level warehouse replenishment time. We have been using one warehouse, the Boston warehouse of Hypo, for illustration. Table 7 displays the effect of customer service level and warehouse replenishment time decisions on the service/cost balance for Hypo's total 25-point distribution system.

TABLE 7

Effect of: Customer Service Level
Replenishment Lead Time
Hypo: 25-Point System

	Customer Service Level		
	80%	*90%*	*95%*
25-day replenishment time			
Total	$6,165,800	$9,079,000	$11,318,000
10-day replenishment time			
Total	$3,790,050	$5,392,300	$ 6,623,750
Difference	$2,375,750	$3,686,700	$ 4,694,250
	80% to 95% C.S.L.—Increased Inventories 70%–85%		
	10- to 25-Day R.T.—Increased Inventories 60%–75%		

Table 7 shows that going from an 80 percent to a 95 percent service level, inventories increase 70–85 percent. Moving from a 10- to a 25-day replenishment time, inventories are increased 60–75 percent. Hypo's selected combination of 90 percent service level with a 10-day replenishment time requires a $5,392,300 inventory.

Hypo system—selective stocking. Table 8 shows the effect of selective stocking, using Hypo's 25-point system with a 90 percent customer service level and a 10-day replenishment time.

Local stocking of all 1,000 items gives the best service and the highest cost. Distribution costs are $1,997,000 with 90 percent first to the third-day delivery. Stocking C and D items at the factory reduces the cost by $674,000 but also provides the poorest service. Hypo management chose to stock A and B items in each distribution point, and C and D items in five regional points located in New York, Indianapolis, San Francisco, Atlanta and Dallas. The cost savings approximate $146,000 with very little reduction in service.

TABLE 8

EFFECT OF: SELECTIVE STOCKING
HYPO: 25-POINT SYSTEM
(90% C.S.L.)
(10-day replenishment time)

	Inventory Investment	Distribution Costs	Delivery Service (Days)	
			1–3	4–10
A. Stocking 1,000 items each point ...	$9,079	$1,997	90%	100%
B. A and B items local C and D items 5 dual: New York, Indianapolis, San Francisco, Atlanta, Dallas....	$8,182	$1,851	88	100
C. A and B items local C and D items factory	$5,118	$1,323	79	100

Local Stocking—Best Service/Highest Cost
C and D Items Factory—Poorest Service/Lowest Cost

DECISION 5: TOTAL SYSTEMS OPTIMIZATION

Now, we have reviewed a typical company, **The Hypo Company**, doing $50 million of annual volume. And we have discussed together four key profit decisions that have a basic and important impact on the profits of The Hypo Company; decisions that should have the attention, not only of marketing people but also the president and other executive officers of the company.

Table 9 portrays the optimization of Hypo's distribution system and the results.

TABLE 9

DISTRIBUTION AND INVENTORY MANAGEMENT
KEY TO PROFITS IN THE SIXTIES
HYPO COMPANY: $50,000,000 ANNUAL VOLUME

Increased Profits

5 Key Profit Decisions:

1. Number of distribution points—100 to 25 points $1,460,000
2. Customer service level, 90%–20% improvement
3. Warehouse replenishment time—25 to 10 days 811,000
4. Selective Stock—5 dual warehouses 146,000

5. Total system optimization $2,417,000

Improved Service—90% Customer Service Level
Balanced Inventory
Total Increased Profits—$2,417,000
(4.8% of Sales)

Decision 1: Number of distribution points. Reducing from 100 to 25 points increases the profits of The Hypo Company per year $1,460,000

Decision 2: Customer service level. 90 percent C.S.L. is a 20 percent service improvement with balanced inventories.

Decision 3: Warehouse replenishment time. Reducing the warehouse replenishment time from 25 to 10 days increases profits .... $ 811,000

Decision 4: Selective stocking. Stocking A and B items in all 25 distribution points and establishing five dual warehouses for the C and D items increases profits .... $ 146,000

Decision 5: Total system optimization. Optimization increases profits annually $2,417,000

Hypo's customer service has been improved 20 percent with balanced inventories. Hypo's total profits increased $2,417,000 or 4.8 percent of sales. Service and cost have been optimized with major improvements in both areas.

2. DISTRIBUTION IDEAS IN A CHANGING MARKET*

Donald C. Nelson

In today's dynamic and changing market there is altogether too often one area of marketing management which is overlooked in keeping an orderly and efficient process of the marketing function within companies —the area of distribution. When considering this subject, we must remember that we are really dealing with two forces—sales distribution and physical distribution.

In sales distribution, we deal with the forces of a customer service program, which includes advertising, sales promotion, and marketing research; in the area of physical distribution, we deal with the logistical forces of transportation, warehousing, inventory control, and material handling. Before continuing, the question may be raised: How long has it been since the firm, if ever, audited its distribution practices? Have the distribution system and practices in the company actually been analyzed carefully to see what cost and time could be saved in improving the firm's efficiency and profit position? Several companies do this on a regularly scheduled basis. They find it is usually the little things pertaining to distribution that they often overlook. When corrected, they can solve several related problems in marketing management.

DISTRIBUTION—NO-MAN'S-LAND

It is often said that management takes the attitude that distribution is the no-man's-land between manufacturing and sales. So long as a sale is made there is little concern at what takes place between

*From *Key to Marketing Progress*, American Marketing Association, Summer, 1963, pp. 427–30.

the manufacturing process and delivery to the customer. In several companies an idea which is used to great success is to keep the distribution department separate from the sales department, thereby allowing marketing management to control the forces of distribution more efficiently. These forces, of course, shape the marketing system in which the environment of distribution must exist. It is my contention, therefore, that distribution success is in the area of management control.

I often find that the primary difference between excellent and average profits is the concern management gives to distribution costs. By means of value analysis, the quality of customer service may be improved while reducing the cost of the program at the same time. Only through this concept can marketing management realistically keep an expanding profit picture.

Consider the forces of support and resistance in the industrial marketing field distribution system and the ideas we can bring out in this analysis. In mature and highly competitive markets the real struggle between companies is in the effective coverage of: (1) geographic area; (2) relations with each customer; and (3) representation of each product line of the company. To take care of this problem a company can choose to have: (1) its own salesmen; (2) company branches; (3) independent distributors; or (4) a combination of these. The idea is to work out an effective representation of market coverage. In any case, it depends upon the product line and the marketing area the company has when management selects its distribution system.

EFFECTIVE DISTRIBUTION CONTROL

One approach which has been applied very effectively is specializing salesmen to be responsible for selling only certain products. This allows each salesman to become a specialist in a particular area, affording more effective market coverage. It is especially useful if technical problems make it difficult for any one salesman to know about several product lines. Also, if the salesman has to sell to different classes of customers, he can perform his job more effectively by having better information pertaining to his specialized area. It is very important, therefore, for industrial marketing management to keep effective control of its field system. In other words, promoting the product line extensively, enforcing certain performance standards of product service, and supplying good technical service to each customer. The strength of an industrial distribution system is determined between the character of the field sales force and the effort made in promoting the product. Thus, control in the company distribution system becomes the key to effective market coverage and better profits.

An outstanding example of effective distribution control is the Macklanburg-Duncan Company of Oklahoma City. This firm is a worldwide manufacturer of building material products which include weather stripping, glazing compounds, aluminum levels, folding doors, and other related lines. Their products are sold to retail warehouses and lumber and building supply dealers. Their sales distribution department is broken down into sales, advertising, product development, and market research; their physical distribution department is broken down into traffic coordination, rates and claims analysis, distribution cost analysis, distribution system analysis, warehouse and materials handling, marketing coordination and purchasing coordination. Effective control is kept on their field distribution by the use of wide-area telephoning, in which the United States is broken down into different districts, and a time schedule is kept on calling each salesman for his report. The call coordinator codes the sales order and relates it onto a data processing control sheet. After all calls are made, this record goes to the data processing center. In this way they keep what is known as instantaneous inventory in their sales effort.

What this company tries to do in all of its organization is: (1) develop a better customer service program, and (2) eliminate handling, which can eventually cut costs. This goes back to the concept of *value analysis* that I mentioned previously. The Macklanburg-Duncan Company has found out that by analyzing on a scheduled basis the individual parts of their distribution system, savings are made by eliminating unnecessary movement and becoming more efficient in the system they are already using. It might be added that this company has become one of the largest manufacturers of building products over a relatively short period of time through the willingness of management to employ up-to-date marketing methods in all areas of organization.

In summary, what I suggest is that the marketing manager in each individual company take a closer look at his distribution process. Is it really performing the job that he wants it to do? Does he know what costs are affecting the distribution process? Does he have a clear picture of the coordinated efforts within his field distribution system? Finally, does he have a short-range and long-range plan to have continued improvements within the distribution framework of his company? These are questions that must surely be answered in today's changing market.

3. SPATIAL AND TEMPORAL ASPECTS OF PHYSICAL DISTRIBUTION*

J. L. Heskett

The title of this paper could well have been shortened to mention only temporal matters related to physical distribution. For the major argument presented is that undue, misplaced emphasis on spatial matters in physical distribution to date has created a major void in the

*From *Marketing and Economic Development,* American Marketing Association, September, 1965, pp. 679-87.

effective measurement of physical distribution activity and the development of more valid management models. Evidence of both a macro- and microeconomic nature will be offered to support this view. A conceptualization of a physical distribution system offering a more valid basis for description and analysis will be presented.

For purposes of discussion the term "spatial" will be used here to refer to characteristics of a physical distribution system described by distance-oriented measures, while the term "temporal" will refer to characteristics described by time-oriented measures. It is not suggested that the terms are mutually exclusive.

MACROECONOMIC SYMPTOMS OF THE PROBLEM

Economists and economic geographers implicity have placed major emphasis on spatial aspects of business beginning with the earliest work in the field.

Von Thünen's studies[1] related to land use in the 16th century were landmarks in two senses of the word. Not only did they mark the beginning but also the direction of work in economic geography for centuries to follow. There was little reason for Von Thünen to be concerned with other than spatial matters in his work. The areas near the city-state which he described by concentric rings emanating from the city center were relatively small, regularly described, and because of regular topography and limited traffic, accessible to the city center in an inverse relation to their distance from it. Von Thünen observed few irregularities in the pattern of agriculture resulting from the displacement of lower income crops by higher income crops on land of increasing value. Assuming that perishability of agricultural products was of limited relevance, or only substantiated the spatial framework of Von Thünen's theory by varying directly with crop value, temporal considerations justifiably were given no emphasis in the theory.

Pursuing our landmarks further, we come to the work of Weber.[2] His relatively rich models of industrial location considered as variables: (1) the nature of raw material components and finished products—that is, whether they were localized or ubiquitous, weight-losing or pure, (2) the relative location of a two-dimensional plane of raw material sources and finished product markets, and (3) the magnitude of labor (production) costs at all possible locations. They assumed that both transportation costs and transit times were linear in relation to distance. If transportation "rates" of Weber's day and in his country were com-

---

[1]Johann Heinrich von Thünen, *Der Isolierte Staat in Beziehung auf Landwirtschaft und Nationalökonomie* (3rd ed.; Berlin: Schumacher-Zarchlin, 1875).

[2]Alfred Weber, *Über den Standort der Industrien* (Tübingen, 1909), translated by C. J. Friedrich as *Alfred Weber's Theory of the Location of Industries* (Chicago: University of Chicago Press, 1929).

parable to ours today, we know that the first part of his assumption is true if we confine ourselves to a single method of transportation and disregard fixed costs. Again, given the regular topography of his models and the limited transport alternatives of his day, it is understandable that he would assume time equated to distance to the extent that temporal aspects of the problem remained unmentioned. This assumption was to continue unduly to influence students of the subject for some time.

Among Weber's successors, various economists with their linear market models[3] and economic geographers of the location theory school neglected even to pay lip service to the model irregularities introduced by varying degrees of accessibility measured in units of time. The work of the latter group exhibits the lengths to which researchers have gone to eliminate aberrations of time in formulating theory. For example, Lösch presumably did not choose the state of Iowa by accident as the area for much of his research in this country.[4] It provided him with a somewhat homogeneous economy, laced regularly with transport arteries, and sufficiently compact and landlocked to rule out most alternative modes of transportation. Only the work of Dean[5] appears to make a limited effort to consider effects of irregular topography and the impact of transportation technology in location, thereby indirectly giving heed to temporal considerations.

Of the regional scientists placing major emphasis on techniques of input-output analysis, a great deal of recent empirical work has been done by Isard. But again, his most extensive published study[6] did not have to deal with temporal aspects of the supply and distribution problem in determining what would be produced and stored where. Those items in the petroleum product family studied in which interregional (international) transportation was a factor were relatively homogeneous. One method of transportation, by water, was feasible. Inventory costs, while a variable, probably were not sufficiently important to influence greatly the results of the analysis.

The concept of accessibility employed by graph theorists suggests

[3]For example, see Harold Hotelling, "Stability in Competition," *Economic Journal,* March, 1929, pp. 41–57; F. Zeuthen, "Theoretical Remarks on Price Policy: Hotelling's Case with Variations," *Quarterly Journal of Economics,* Vol. 47, pp. 231–53, and Edward H. Chamberlin, *The Theory of Monopolistic Competition* (3rd ed.; Cambridge, Mass.: Harvard University Press, 1938), Appendix C.

[4]August Lösch, *Die Räumliche Ordnung der Wirtschaft* (Jena: Gustav Fischer Verlag, 1940), translated from the second revised edition (1944) by William H. Woglom with the assistance of Wolfgang F. Stopler, *The Economics of Location* (New Haven: Yale University Press, 1954).

[5]William H. Dean, Jr., *The Theory of the Geographic Location of Economic Activities, Selections from the Doctoral Dissertation* (Ann Arbor: Edwards Brothers, Inc., 1938).

[6]Walter Isard, Eugene W. Schooler, and Thomas Vietoriaz, *Industrial Complex Analysis and Regional Development* (New York and Cambridge, Mass.: John Wiley & Sons, Inc., and The Technology Press of the Massachusetts Institute of Technology, 1959), see especially pp. 96–97.

the opportunity for the eventual use of time rather than distance in its computation. However, thus far major studies of this type have concerned the impact of alternative network investments on cumulative nodal accessibility for transportation networks containing only one mode of transport.[7] At such time as they are developed to the point where transportation systems describing modes with widely varying characteristics are superimposed upon one another, a consideration of cumulative times rather than distances in measuring the degree of accessibility inherent in various systems and system combinations will be necessary.

Only urban geographers appear to have placed some emphasis on temporal aspects of distribution on a somewhat macroeconomic level.[8] This is natural, because the subject commodity of their location studies has invariably been people. Because of its importance to him, the commuter or shopper measures distance in minutes, not miles. His location decision, and consequently the face of the community, is altered by the factor of time.

This is by no means a complete list of examples; nor is it meant to be bibliographically complete. Writers singled out were selected not necessarily because of their prominence in their field, but because of the representative nature of their work. Further, the major intent of this discussion has not been to criticize the work of economists and economic geographers concerned with spatial aspects of economic activity. For one reason or another, each had good reason not to be concerned about temporal aspects of his problem which might otherwise have been an influence on costs. Attempts to neutralize the impact of time in supply and distribution perhaps stemmed from a recognition of the problems which might arise from its inclusion in an analysis. However, the work of these men has in some measure confused the issues related to system design at the microeconomic level.

MICROECONOMICS OF SPACE AND TIME

The microeconomics of physical distribution systems concern two major cost categories, transportation and inventory. The former are incurred in the connecting links on a distribution network. The latter are experienced primarily at system nodes, but also while goods are in transit. The proportion contributed by these categories to the total cost of physical distribution in the economy of the United States is approxi-

---

[7]For representative works see William L. Garrison, "Connectivity of the Interstate Highway System," in *Papers and Proceedings* (Philadelphia: Regional Science Association, 1960), pp. 122–37; and Karel Kansky, *Structure of Transportation Networks*, Department of Geography Research Paper No. 84 (Chicago: University of Chicago Press, 1963).

[8]For example, see Lowdon Wingo, Jr., *Transportation and Urban Land* (Washington, D.C.: Resources for the Future, Inc., 1961), especially pp. 43–62; and David L. Huff, "Defining and Estimating a Trading Area," *Journal of Marketing*, July, 1964, pp. 34–38.

mately two thirds for transportation and one third for inventory maintenance, totalling roughly $90 billion, or nearly 24 percent of the gross national product of tangible goods, in 1964.[9]

These major cost areas have spawned a number of models which can be grouped into related categories. Transportation costs in combination with volumes of goods in movement typically have provided the heart of location models, whether the model employed a linear programming, center of gravity, or some other approach. On the other hand, inventory models have directly concerned inventory costs. If you will grant me this much, I would like to make two points in the remainder of the paper:

1. Location models have been spatially oriented to date, while inventory models have been and will always be temporally oriented.
2. A physical distribution system can be described completely for analytic purposes in terms only of its inventories but not in terms only of its transportation elements. If an integrated, accurate method of analyzing physical distribution systems is to be developed, time instead of space will be the relevant unifying dimension to be used. This suggests that the proper approach to the construction of an integrated model must combine the elements of a temporally-oriented location model and an inventory model.

ORIENTATION OF LOCATION AND INVENTORY MODELS

The most popular approaches to location problems thus far have been spatially oriented. The center of gravity method has typically sought to minimize ton-miles accumulated between supply and demand points on a system. Where varying rates have applied to the ton-miles involved, a weighted ton-mile measure has been used. Nevertheless, with one exception that I am aware of—Bowersox's use of transit time between a grocery warehouse and retail outlets in an urban setting[10]— the object of center of gravity models has been to minimize distance rather than time.

Linear programming models for location have invariably employed transportation costs between potential system nodes.[11] To the extent that transportation costs are assumed to be linear in relation to distance, this is a spatial measure. Finally, in the most extensively used heuristic programming models, distance is again the factor employed to describe nodal relationships, if published accounts of past effects are indicative of current work.[12]

---

[9]Author's estimate.

[10]Donald J. Bowersox, "An Analytical Approach to Warehouse Location," *Handling & Shipping*, February, 1962, pp. 17–20.

[11]See for example William J. Baumol and Philip Wolfe, "A Warehouse Location Problem," *Operations Research*, March–April, 1958, pp. 252–63.

[12]Alfred A. Kuehn and Michael J. Hamburger, "A Heuristic Program for Locating Warehouses," *Management Science*, July, 1963, pp. 643–66.

Inventory models, in contrast, have no spatial orientation in the context of the definition of the term given earlier. The relationship of a demand point to its supply point is stated in terms of time for all models allowing uncertainty. And of course, the relevant time is not transit time between inventory locations but the order cycle time required to complete the course of communications and order shipment extending from the point of order to the supply point and back again to the point of delivery.

CONCEPTUALIZATION OF THE PHYSICAL DISTRIBUTION SYSTEM

All distances can be described in terms of the time required to traverse them, whether the transmissions are of messages, people, or goods. Of course, a range of times (each with its cost) can be associated with every distance. If so described, this makes the measurement of distance usually associated with location models dimensionally consistent with the relevant inputs necessary for inventory models under conditions of uncertainty. These, of course, include carrying costs, ordering cost, and stock-out costs in addition to order cycle times.

In total, a physical distribution system can be described in terms of its inventories and their determinants. But this requires a description of inventories in transit as well as at nodal points on a network. Thus, a system of three plants, two distribution warehouses, and ten markets arranged as in Figure 1 can be conceived of as having anywhere from 26 to 45 inventory "cells" of all or some goods in a product line.

Some aspects of these cells should be elaborated on in passing. Momentarily, any one cell may be empty. Over time, all contain something. The elimination of a warehouse in configuration A of Figure 1 would eliminate not one but 15 inventories and probably affect many of the remaining 30.

You'll notice, too, that the networks in Figure 1 are dimensionless. Both distance and time prove to be unsatisfactory dimensions for the graphic description of a physical distribution system. The shortcomings of distance as a measure have been discussed. Time as a determinant of inventory levels in various cells is a promising but confusing measure, for it takes on different meanings for inventories in transit as opposed to those at nodal points.

The level of in-transit inventories is directly influenced by, among other things, transit times between a given set of nodes in a system. A different time period, that required for the completion of an order cycle, is relevant for a determination of the inventory level at a nodal point.[13]

The first of these assertions requires a reevaluation of the assumption implicit in most location models that in the location of one or more

---

[13]Bowersox hints at this in his paper, "Total Information Systems in Logistics," in J. L. Heskett (ed.), *Business Logistics—Appraisal and Prospect* (Stanford, Cal.: Stanford University Graduate School of Business, 1965), pp. 109-22.

FIGURE 1

DESIGNATION OF INVENTORY CELLS IN TWO ALTERNATIVE SYSTEMS
FOR PHYSICALLY DISTRIBUTING GOODS FROM THREE PLANTS
THROUGH TWO DISTRIBUTION WAREHOUSES TO TEN MARKETS

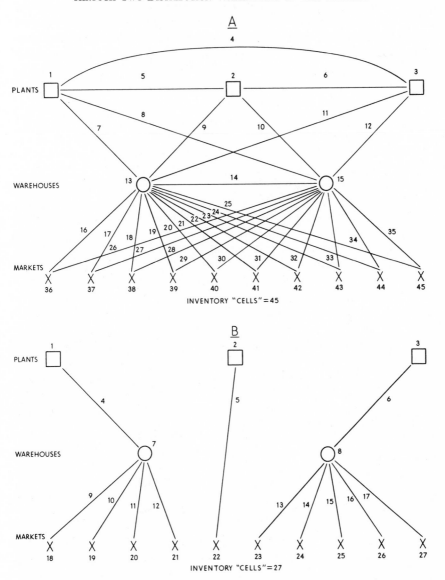

facilities on a network, a minimization of total distance between relevant existing nodes and the proposed nodes (least ton-mile points) will somehow lead to minimum transit times. As has been suggested, where various transport methods can be employed to traverse a given distance, neither time nor cost may bear a close relationship to distance.

The relevance of order cycle times to nodal inventories, on the other hand, requires an examination of the implicit assumption (stretched one step further) that distances between network nodes are somehow related to order cycle times for goods ordered and shipped between them. The rationale for the assumption logically might be the direct relationships between distance and transit time on the one hand and transit time and order cycle time on the other. However, time in transit represents roughly only 40 percent of total order cycle time according to available studies.[14] Further, in a sample of means of order cycle times for two categories of products, which we carefully measured several years ago, the relationship between order cycle times and distances for shipments moving from various manufacturers to a distribution warehouse was so low as to be almost meaningless. Specifically, the coefficients of determination were .11 and .16 for drug and candy and tobacco products, respectively.[15]

One additional argument for the lack of relevance of transport-oriented location models for the real problem of physical distribution system design can be advanced. With one exception, location models devised to date have had cost minimization as their sole objective. The one exception with which I am familiar is that reported by Mossman and Morton in which the effect of location on service and hence demand is explored in the context of a traditional location model.[16] Unless demand is assumed constant regardless of system design, cost minimization has little to do with profit maximization in a physical distribution system. Further, the costs minimized in available spatial models are often not inclusive of all those incurred in physical distribution.

The time-oriented inventory model, in contrast, considers order-cycle time and dependability as two of the determinants of demand. By relating both demand (revenue) and costs, this type of model lends itself more easily to a description of a profit-maximization objective than spatial models.

SUMMARY AND CONCLUSION

In summary, our concentration on spatial relationships in physical distribution, while the product of several hundred years of effort in the

---

[14]Evidence of this is presented in Richard A. Johnson and Donald D. Parker, "Optimizing Customer Delivery Service with Improved Distribution," *Business Review*, October, 1961, pp. 38–46, at p. 44; and Paul R. Stephenson, "Manufacturers' Physical Distribution Service Knowledge and Penalties: An Experimental Analysis," an unpublished Master's thesis deposited in the library of The Ohio State University, 1963.

[15]Unpublished research by the author in collaboration with John Rider and Paul R. Stephenson.

[16]Frank H. Mossman and Newton Morton, *Logistics of Distribution Systems* (Boston: Allyn and Bacon, Inc., 1965), pp. 245–56.

formulation of macroeconomic theory, has not yielded a valid, comprehensive approach to the description and analysis of physical distribution systems. Several reasons for this have been advanced. First, temporal relationships assumed in spatially-oriented location models are not valid. These assumptions are unnecessary in an inventory model with time as one dimension. Second, spatial models have as their objective the minimization of transport costs only. While considering only inventory carrying costs to date, the temporal inventory model offers more opportunity for a comprehensive treatment of all physical distribution costs. Third, location models have had as their objective the minimization of costs. Temporally oriented approaches have emphasized the more valid objective of profit maximization.

This suggests that a physical distribution system can be viewed most productively as a set of actual or potential inventory cells linked and partially determined by time—transit time for those inventory cells in network links, order cycle time for those cells at network nodes. A shift in emphasis from spatial to temporal aspects of physical distribution will hopefully lead to an analytic approach devoid of crippling assumptions, all-inclusive in its consideration of system costs, and aimed at the maximization of profits.

4. THE ROLE OF PHYSICAL DISTRIBUTION IN MARKETING ORGANIZATION*

Edward W. Smykay

Just a few short years ago, only a few lonely voices extolled the virtues of physical distribution management. Today, there appears a new awareness of its potent effect on efficient and profitable operations. Top management no longer seeks a "Goldmine in Transit" as once reported in *Dun's Review* but, rather, searches for diamonds in distribution.

Three major problems in implementing known principles of distribution analysis are: 1) structuring effective organization, 2) discovering applicable methods, and 3) finding properly qualified personnel. These three components are interwoven into a single fabric, and any attempt to treat them separately results in ineffective implementation. Proper recognition of such interrelations must begin with a definition of the field of physical distribution.

Since there appears some difference of opinion as to the proper definition of physical distribution management, I shall propose my own. Physical distribution management is the emerging business science which deals with the control of material flows through a facilities network. By

*From *Effective Marketing Coordination*, American Marketing Association, June, 1961, pp. 387–92.

this definition, included are all materials in motion and all storage facilities except those directly related to production. It follows naturally that the main components of physical distribution are: 1) transportation, and 2) storage. Without control of these two key areas and their subsidiary elements, integrated management of this function is impossible.

The main elements of any science are: 1) a systematic body of knowledge, 2) numerical expression of data, and 3) established principles showing the interrelationship of data. A science contains a set of laws useful in developing procedures and designing experiments. The importance of this point to physical distribution is that there currently exists a body of laws useful in analyzing alternative systems of action in a distribution network in the same fashion as any experimental science.

IMPORTANCE OF PHYSICAL DISTRIBUTION

It is now well established that the cost of manufacturing a product is less than the cost of moving raw materials to plant and finished products to customers. Recent studies show that manufacturing costs account for only 41 percent of final consumer prices, while nonmanufacturing costs account for 59 percent. Of these nonmanufacturing costs, physical distribution is likely the largest cost of doing business in most firms. While substantial cost reduction may continue to occur as a result of improved production methods, potential savings in physical distribution lead to its correlative importance to more glamorous product manufacture.

Cost categories of this important function include: 1) investment in fixed facilities such as warehouses; 2) transportation expense, 3) packaging, and 4) inventory cost of goods in the distribution pipeline. The freight bill alone amounted to about $40 billion in 1959. In my own experience, this cost category represents anywhere from one fourth to one sixth of total physical distribution cost. If this reflects average experience, physical distribution expense in the United States amounts to somewhere between $160 billion and $240 billion. A 1 percent reduction in this cost category can conceivably increase business profits in this country by as much as $2.4 billion. For those companies doing nothing in analyzing their physical distribution costs, reductions of at least 10 percent are, generally, easily attainable.

PHYSICAL DISTRIBUTION AS A SYSTEM

In the systems concept, attention is focused upon the total action of a function rather than upon its individual components. One illustration may clarify the point. Traffic department reports of a few years ago indicate that attention was generally focused on savings in transportation. Indicated savings, in fact, frequently reflected real savings to the firm; perhaps just as frequently, they were illusory.

For example, one major method of reducing transportation charges is to consolidate shipments into large lots. But such consolidation tends to cause delay in shipping schedules, thus adversely affecting inventory levels. Conceivably, such delays may result in inventory cost increases actually greater than freight rate reductions, thus increasing total distribution cost. Given product value, consolidation delays, freight rate schedules, and time in transit, the actual distribution costs via alternative shipping schedules is determinable.

In the above simple cases, the dangers of fragmented organization are illustrated. When each cost center is analyzed separately, it is entirely possible and probable that, while cost in each center is independently minimized, the total cost of the entire system is not at all minimized.

In this connection, it may be indicated here that the profit-and-loss statement, geared to profit accounting, and the balance sheet, designed to estimate financial position, are of little practical value in physical distribution analysis. Traditional accounting systems are rarely appropriate to the kind of analysis needed; such analysis thus requires a high number of special studies transcending the limits of present accounting practice.

METHODS USED IN PHYSICAL DISTRIBUTION

Marketing orientation places greater reliance on logistic support, which leads directly to a more important role for transport control than results from production orientation. "Gray areas" of responsibility abound in a production-oriented firm; a market orientation, on the other hand, provides the long bench which permits the rational collection of these responsibilities and prevents their "falling between the chairs."

Available studies on physical distribution suggest three types of orientation: 1) transportation, 2) engineering, and 3) mathematics.

In the engineering approach, great effort is expended toward facilities improvements. New materials handling methods, loading and unloading devices, changed boxcar and trailer designs, and other such mechanical innovations of a predominantly engineering type are the central theme of this approach.

With transportation orientation, shipping schedules, transport selection, and rate adjustments overshadow other considerations. In some cases, rather sophisticated approaches are employed in solving this class of problems.

Mathematical model building requires a reconstruction of physical flows of materials and goods through the entire network of distribution and transportation facilities. Representative types of mathematical methods used in this type of analysis include: 1) simulation, 2) linear programming, and 3) synthetic cost analysis.

PERSONNEL

Dynamic growth in the complex development of American business raises serious issue of sources of executive supply generally. Forecasts of the supply of budding executives in the age group 35–45 indicate that, for the next 10 years, the number of persons in this age group will remain virtually constant as a result of scarcity. Business recruiting practices in the colleges have been significantly altered from a mere search for bodies to a highly competitive market for top talent. All indications are that present scarcities of executive talent are a long-run phenomenon and not a temporary condition.

Given this competitive environment, the question arises as to where skilled distribution analysts shall come from. Most probably they will come from present executive pools in traffic, purchasing, marketing, and industrial engineering. But this will occur only among the few who are trained in modern mathematics and who also have an appreciation of the total system of materials and product flows in a marketing environment.

The second source of supply is among the few universities presently offering formal academic training in physical distribution. To my personal knowledge, Michigan State University, the institution which I presently represent, was the first university to offer formal academic programs related to physical distribution. Our first course in this area was offered five years ago and now consists of three closely related courses covering practically all of the critical places of the field. In addition, supporting courses in marketing, economics, packaging, purchasing, and others are offered. Those graduating from this program are in high demand for both academic and industrial positions. There is abundant evidence that other universities will soon follow with programs of their own design.

In addition to formal academic programs, there are now in existence a number of short courses in continuing education for executives. Among these, the American Management Association has been in the forefront as indicated by today's program. These, I am sure, will continue to grow in abundance and variety so that gearing up for expert performance in the complex field of physical distribution will be eased as a result.

ORGANIZATION OF THE DISTRIBUTION FUNCTIONS

Any attempt to prescribe in detail an organization structure to fit all situations is foredoomed to failure. Existing organization structures, available personnel, and individual corporate objectives all act to temper any ideal organizational arrangement.

The reality of existing facts transmutes the empty boxes and straight

lines of organization charts to vitally operating organisms. The fundamental asset of any company in assessing its future potential lies more
with its people than with the mere formalism of organization charts,
balance sheets, profit-and-loss statements, and other paraphernalia of
corporate life.

Rather than attempt to define an organizational structure in detail,
I prefer to outline the main elements of a distribution program. From
this, an organization may be tailored to suit existing circumstances of
particular companies. These main elements are:

1. Make market forecasts by regions, states, Standard Metropolitan
   Areas, counties, and cities.
2. Set inventory levels to satisfy market demand within the limits of
   an agreed-upon customer service level.
3. Establish production requirements to meet finished product and inventory standards.
4. Establish most economical sources of supply with reference to their
   locations and associated cost of movement.
5. Determine the appropriate number of warehouses to achieve minimum cost within prescribed service limits.
6. Establish a communications system to control flows of materials
   through facilities.
7. Analyze packaging requirements.
8. Select transport alternatives.
9. Choose materials handling systems for distribution facilities.
10. Determine most economic shipping patterns.
11. Determine most profitable market areas.
12. Coordinate sales and promotion with logistic support.
13. Set order-process and order-pick methods.
14. Influence plant location decisions.
15. Determine warehouse locations.
16. Make studies of raw material and product flows.

CONCLUSION

In conclusion, I wish to say that the organization of the physical distribution function depends on: 1) availability of personnel trained in
the field; 2) present orientation of the corporation, whether outwardly
to marketing or inwardly to production, and 3) acceptability of the importance of this area of business on the part of the chief executive
officer.

While in some cases strong centralized control over the physical distribution is possible and desirable, in others a loose cooperative arrangement is more suitable. In any case, whether a single head or a coopera-

tive method is selected to control all of the function, fragmentary and individual control must be avoided at all cost. A fragmented approach to this peculiar function leads only to no control of it at all.

5. IMPROVED EFFICIENCY AND REDUCED COST IN MARKETING*

Donald D. Parker

The Committee on Definitions of the American Marketing Association defines "marketing" as follows: "The performance of business activities that direct the flow of goods and services from producer to consumer or user."[1]

No attempt is made to challenge this definition. Instead, it is presented here to point out that marketing encompasses activities much broader than selling, sales promotion, and marketing research. Emphasis on these functions in current popular business literature has resulted, unfortunately, in a restricted concept of the scope and status of marketing activities in industry.

Marketing management is the exercise of proper management controls over *all* the business functions implied in the above definition. Marketing management, therefore, is much broader than sales management. It includes the exchange functions of buying and selling, the physical distribution functions of transportation and storage, and the other functions which facilitate marketing—such as financing, risk bearing, and communication.

Substantial progress has been made in improving the efficiency and reducing the cost of production and manufacturing activities. These improvements are major contributors to increased standards of living in the United States. Although we are far from ultimate efficiency in production, there is little doubt that progress there has outstripped improved efficiency in marketing activities.

Yet consumers pay for lost motions in the management and integration of marketing activities as surely as they pay for inefficiency in production. Society can no more afford inefficiency in marketing than it can afford wasteful methods of production; the social cost is no less real. Likewise, companies which fail to improve the efficiency of their distribution activities will fall behind in our competitive economy.

Journal of Marketing, April, 1962, pp. 15–21.
[1]Ralph S. Alexander and others, *Marketing Definition: A Glossary of Marketing Terms* (Chicago: American Marketing Association, 1960), p. 15.

THE NEW MARKETING CONCEPT

A significant trend in American industry today is the increased attention being paid to marketing activities by top management. Seldom has
business management indulged in such critical examination as is prevalent today in the marketing field.

Companies of all sizes are conducting searching inquiries into consumer habits and motivations, in attempts to determine what they can
do to develop or maintain leadership in the marketplace. Serious thought
is being given to the proper integration of marketing with the other
divisions of the company. Marketing personnel gradually are playing a
more important role in product development and production scheduling.

In short, more emphasis is being placed on learning more about the
needs, wants, desires, likes, and dislikes of customers and using this
knowledge as a primary basis for planning and organizing the entire
operations of companies. Significant steps are being taken to improve
the efficiency and reduce the costs of performing marketing activities.
In far too many cases the steps being taken are restricted only to the
marketing research, selling, and sales promotion aspects of marketing
and fail to include the other marketing functions. Until all marketing
activities are integrated and until all marketing costs are considered,
the potential for improved efficiency and cost reduction cannot be
realized.

THE COST-PRICE SQUEEZE

A recent survey conducted by Dun and Bradstreet asked American
business leaders to indicate what they consider to be the most crucial
issues facing industry in the 1960's.[2] Responses were received from 1,225
large companies. Many factors were mentioned, but the issue specified
most often as most crucial was the "cost-price squeeze" by 27 percent
of the manufacturers and 23 percent of all the respondents. Other issues
—such as taxes, international tensions, and inflation—which have been
dominant in the past are considered relatively less crucial today.

Whenever any company faces a squeeze between the costs of doing
business and the prices at which they sell, the alternatives for survival
are extremely limited. The pattern of prices usually is set by competition, with leadership often assumed by the most efficient competitors.
The elasticity of demand or competitors' prices limit the ability of most
companies to solve the "cost-price squeeze" problem by price changes.
The remaining major alternative is to attack the costs of doing business

---

[2]"News from Dun and Bradstreet, Inc.," Dun and Bradstreet, Inc., November,
1960, pp. 2–5.

in an attempt to improve efficiency and reduce costs. These costs may be classified roughly as production costs and marketing costs; and each constitutes about half of the total cost of doing business.

THE LAST FRONTIER FOR COST ECONOMIES

Unfortunately, improvements in marketing efficiency and reductions in marketing costs still lie in the future, representing a major frontier for cost economies. Too many marketing activities do not lend themselves readily to cost reduction, because they are not repetitive and machines cannot be substituted for the human element.

However, there is room for substantial improvement, particularly in the performance of the physical distribution functions of marketing which constitute a major part of total marketing costs and which are selected for emphasis in this article.

PHYSICAL DISTRIBUTION COSTS

Physical distribution costs are those costs associated with the physical movement of goods. The finished goods of a manufacturer or producer—which may be component parts, raw materials, or expendable supplies for another manufacturer—must be moved and usually stored before they have economic value or utility.

There is a tendency to think of the costs of physical distribution as being comprised of transportation and warehousing costs only. Actually, however, there are other significant costs which must be considered when attempting to analyze and improve physical distribution activities. The nature of these costs varies with different companies, but the following list includes the most common costs associated with physical distribution:

1. Transportation by common carrier, contract carrier, or company-owned equipment
2. Warehousing in public or private facilities
3. Order handling, including back orders
4. Packing
5. Inventory insurance
6. Inventory taxes
7. Inventory handling
8. Inventory obsolescence
9. Inventory capital costs

It is regrettable that the accounting systems of most companies do not permit an accurate determination of these costs individually. Without this determination, it is extremely difficult to evaluate the alternative methods of performing the physical distribution functions. Also, it should be apparent that any steps that can be taken to reduce the amount of inventory have an immediate and significant effect upon physical distribution costs.

THE IMPORTANT COST

These comments about alternative methods of performing physical distribution functions imply that there are varying levels of cost for each alternative. Normally, for example, companies select one or more modes of freight transportation from several alternatives with different costs. Goods may be stored in public or private warehouses. Inventories may be stored centrally or in a varying number of regional warehouses. Various systems for the handling of orders and back orders are available; different types of packing methods and materials are considered before decisions are made. The prevailing practice is for these alternatives to be weighed and decisions reached which will result in the greatest efficiency and least cost in the performance of each particular subfunction, without regard for the effect of those decisions on the cost of performing other related functions.

Yet the mode of transportation selected affects the cost of packing materials to be used. The location of inventories influences the number of times inventories are handled and the attendant costs. Several of these decisions are related to the amount of inventory required to provide a desired level of customer service; thus, they affect the costs associated with inventories.

The most important cost, and the cost on which attention should be focused in any attempt to improve efficiency and reduce costs, is *the total cost of performing the physical distribution activity*—not the separate costs of the individual segments. In other words, it is a mistake to concentrate on reducing the cost of one factor only—such as transportation—when to do so has the effect of increasing the cost of another factor by an amount greater than the amount saved. Conversely, it is wise from the standpoint of improved efficiency and reduced marketing costs to increase one cost if, by decreasing other related costs, the net effect is to reduce the total cost of physical distribution.

ORGANIZATIONAL STRUCTURE AND
FUNCTIONAL DECISIONS

All companies are organized to "manage" physical distribution activities. Most companies place the responsibility for cost and service control at the functional level (for example, traffic manager); and the opportunity to look at the total cost is clouded by divided responsibility. Pressures are applied by top management which encourage the separate functional units to control and reduce their costs of operation. Cost reduction becomes the primary way for these functional units to call attention to themselves. Usually, this means taking steps to optimize the particular functions delegated to them.

Thus, the traffic manager, for example, is motivated to arrange transportation services at the lowest possible cost—which usually means concentration on large quantity shipments by truckload or carload lots. Those delegated responsibility for production planning and production scheduling, likewise, think in terms of minimizing unit production costs. As a result, these and other functions are performed without sufficient regard for the effect of these decisions on other related costs or the total cost. In other words, the optimization of these subfunctions may result in the creation of excessive costs associated with inventory accumulation, inventory control, inventory obsolescence, and warehousing.

The tendency of most companies has been to overlook the potentials for improving service and reducing the total cost of distribution, by failing to coordinate and integrate this responsibility at a higher level in the organizational structure of the company.

The result is a condition of suboptimization—a condition of apparent efficiency in the various parts, but less than optimum efficiency in the operation of the integrated whole. As a result, when decisions are made about transportation, warehousing, packing, inventory levels, and the other factors mentioned, they are based on an analysis of alternatives within that specific function, without regard for the possible effects upon other closely related functions. Functional costs are considered, but the all-important total cost of the related functions is ignored. The need, obviously, is for the creation of a position with responsibility for coordinating the activities of these various functions and controlling the total cost.

Recently several companies have given serious consideration to revising their organizational structure to achieve more efficient integration of the physical distribution functions. For example, the major appliance division of Westinghouse Electric Corporation last year created a new position titled manager, marketing administration. The responsibility of the executive in this position is to integrate traffic, warehousing, order servicing, inventory control, and production scheduling.

Before anything really effective can be done to implement the total cost concept and the desired degree of integration, it must have the full support of the chief executive officer of the company. Otherwise, the necessary realignment of responsibility to make it an effective concept will probably never come to pass. The incentive for interest on the part of top management is a desire for improved control over service and cost. Improved control over service leads to expanded markets . . . improved control over costs leads to a lower total cost of distribution . . . and both lead to a competitive advantage and increased profit.

THE FUNCTION OF INVENTORIES

SERVICE V. COSTS

While inventories of finished goods may result from steps taken to stabilize production or to produce economically, the basic function of inventory accumulation is to provide service to customers. In any competitive market, ready availability of inventory plays an important role in customer service, with the critical problem arising in determining the proper balance between service and the cost of providing service. From the extreme viewpoint of maximum service, complete inventories should be immediately available to all customers and potential customers. To provide this level of service, however, would entail unreasonable costs.

The solution, therefore, must be a compromise in an attempt to offer a reasonable level of service—in light of competition—without incurring excessive costs of carrying, storing, handling, and transporting inventories, and without suffering excessive costs of inventory depreciation and obsolescence.

INVENTORY PROBLEMS

In attempting to find the optimum balance between service to customers and inventory costs, many problems arise. No predetermined solutions are available for any industry or company because of substantial differences in inventory variety, the breadth of the market, the urgency of rapid service, the degree of competition, and other factors. Each company should analyze its particular situation and weigh the factors of service and costs which will lead them to an optimum solution.

In analyzing inventory problems, one important factor is the relative rate of flow of different items held in inventory. Studies of the product lines of various industries show a common pattern of varying volume for different classes of items. Typically, a small percentage of items—usually about 10 percent—account for a high percentage of sales volume —usually about 80 percent. About half of the items account for a very small percentage of sales volume. This is a critical factor because the slow-moving items usually cause much more than their proportionate share of inventory costs (investment, handling costs, insurance, taxes, and obsolescence).

ALTERNATIVES

In most cases, a wide variety of alternatives is available in attempting to optimize inventory location decisions, with each alternative having a different pattern of costs.

Also of importance is the time factor—the time required for inventory delivery from various locations. Different combinations of inventory location and modes of transportation may result in approximately the same time factor, but quite different costs. For example, one company may use inexpensive means of transportation to deliver inventories to a large number of regional warehouses, in order to provide a rapid service to its local markets. Another company may centralize its inventories and use faster and more expensive means of transportation, to provide the same level of service to their customers. The former company will have relatively low transportation costs, with relatively high costs of warehousing, handling, and other costs associated with greater inventory levels. The latter company is providing the same service with reduced inventory, but with relatively high transportation costs. The important factors are the levels of service maintained and the total cost of maintaining that service—not the cost of any particular segment.

In the above example, assuming comparable levels of service to customers, the company with the lower total cost is performing the physical distribution function more efficiently. There is nothing sacred about the maintenance of regional inventories if their elimination or reduction can be accomplished without reducing the level of service to customers.

TOOLS TO FACILITATE PROGRESS

Future progress in improving the efficiency and reducing the cost of performing physical distribution functions lies, first, in the integration and cordination of the several subfunctions which comprise physical distribution activities; and, second, in reducing the time required for the performance of these activities.

Much of the inefficiency and excessive cost prevalent in American industry today is traceable to the suboptimization which results from a failure to view physical distribution activities as a whole. The time lag between order origination and merchandise delivery is the critical factor in matters of customer service, inventory requirements, and the cost of physical distribution.

The solution to problems of maintaining or improving service to customers with reduced inventories lies in reducing the time required for the flow of information and the flow of materials or inventories.

OPERATIONS RESEARCH

The concepts and techniques of operations research have a great deal to offer in any attempt to integrate the subfunctions and reach decisions about physical distribution activities as a whole.[3] The progress of operations researchers in areas of marketing has been slow because of se-

---

[3]As to the application of operations research concepts to marketing, see John F. Magee, "Operations Research in Making Marketing Decisions," *Journal of Marketing,* Vol. 25 (October, 1960), pp. 18-23.

mantic difficulties and lack of familiarity with the nature of marketing problems; but the future looks bright for substantial improvements in marketing efficiency traceable to the application of operations research techniques. The fundamental contributions of operations research to the solution of marketing problems lie in the following areas:

1. *The systems concept*—considering the elements of related business activities as a coordinated whole instead of a group of independent and unrelated elements. The application of this concept to the sub-functions of physical distribution shows substantial promise for improved efficiency and reduced cost.
2. *The model concept*—which has specific application to the preliminary testing of possible alternatives, in search for improved efficiency and cost reduction in physical distribution activities.
3. *Emphasis on experimentation*—without which few companies can reach optimum solutions to physical distribution problems.

Operations researchers are becoming aware of the extreme complexities of marketing activities and the close relationships among the various marketing functions. The foundations have been built for their effective collaboration with management people responsible for marketing efficiency.

In marketing, the greatest success of operations research has been in problems of inventory control, warehouse locations, and other areas related to physical distribution. Out of this success is growing the basis for additional contributions in systems concepts, experimental concepts, and models. Improvement in these areas is the key to the contribution operations research can make to future marketing strategy.

ELECTRONIC DATA PROCESSING

Much of future progress lies in possibilities of reducing the time required for performance of physical distribution activities. This includes reducing the information flow time. Communications in a physical distribution system form the nervous system, providing the feedback necessary to control the system and provide service to customers. Any attempt to reduce the material flow time must be accompanied by corresponding reductions in the information flow time in order to retain balance in the system.

Recent developments and improvements in the capabilities of data transmission and processing equipment have increased tremendously the speed and accuracy of handling greater volumes of data. Progress in reducing the time required for the physical flow of materials actually has lagged behind the advances made in the area of information flow. High-speed electronic computers have made it possible for companies to deal with much larger quantities of information. Increased speeds allow companies to process data which heretofore were unusable.

In addition, computers have stimulated the rethinking of whole new systems of information flow by progressive management personnel. More information may be received; it may be received more rapidly; it may be processed more rapidly; and it may be processed in new and different ways for purposes of better control and improved efficiency.

AIRFREIGHT

Recent developments and impending improvements in the airfreight industry represent interesting possibilities for companies interested in reducing material flow time—with reduced inventory requirements and costs—as a means of improving the efficiency and reducing the total cost of physical distribution.[4]

Throughout business history, whenever a new mode of freight transportation is introduced, it has developed slowly because the relative cost has been higher. Usually it is considered to be a premium means of transportation, to be used only in cases of emergency. Then gradually the new mode of transportation expands, improves the quality of service offered, and reaches a point of mass acceptance as a routine mover of freight. In each case, the effect has been to revolutionize business practices, particularly in the area of physical distribution.

Today the airfreight industry is in the latter phases of its introductory period, but is approaching rapidly a breakthrough to widespread acceptance as a routine mode of freight transportation. The growth of airfreight during the post-World War II period has been quite spectacular, but still represents only a tiny portion of 1 percent of the total ton-miles of intercity freight movement. Only in a very few cases is airfreight considered to be other than a form of transportation to be used in extreme emergency or when unusual speed of delivery is all-important. Although airfreight rates have declined substantially, they still are much higher than rates for surface transportation. The quality reputation of airfreight has suffered from erratic and inconsistent service, and from too many examples of unreliability.

Most of the problems which have resulted in damaging the service reputation of the airfreight industry are traceable to (1) the fact that airfreight has been carried in craft not designed specifically for this purpose; and (2) the fact that the bulk of airfreight has been carried aboard passenger airplanes in which passenger operations receive top priority and airfreight is incidental.

With regard to improvements in airfreight equipment, steps are being taken which indicate that the future picture is bright. The CL-44, a large turboprop airplane designed specifically for all-cargo operation, has been built by Canadair, a subsidiary of General Dynamics, in Mon-

---

[4]George M. Shutes, "Airfreight from a Marketing Viewpoint," *Journal of Marketing*, Vol. 25 (October, 1960), pp. 39-43.

treal. Delivery of these airplanes to the Flying Tiger Line, Slick Airways, and Seaboard and Western Airline began in 1961. Other airlines have converted airplanes for all-cargo use during the interim period before they place orders for more efficient all-cargo craft.

The spread between airfreight rates and rates for surface transportation is destined to become smaller and smaller. The trend in rates for surface freight transportation is upward, while airfreight rates are being reduced. Rates charged by rail and truck carriers have increased sharply during the post-World War II period, and there are indications that this trend will continue in the future.

On the other hand, the trend in airfreight rates is downward, and there are growing indications of declines in the very near future. The inauguration of service by the new and more efficient aircraft will result in decreases in the cost of providing airfreight service. Impending use of new terminals and new cargo-handling equipment, when combined with anticipated increases in volume, will add to the pressures for reduced rates.

Airfreight, particularly in light of impending improvements in service and reduction in rates, offers an opportunity for many companies to reduce their material flow time. Increased use of airfreight may be related directly to maintaining or improving service to customers with reduced inventory and reduced total costs of performing the physical distribution function. Deterrents have been the relative cost of airfreight, the service reputation of airfreight, and the failure of companies to conceive of their physical distribution as an integrated whole. Most of these deterrents will vanish in the future.

THE RAYTHEON CASE

Several companies and governmental units have taken steps to reduce information and material flow time as a means of reducing both inventory levels and total cost of physical distribution, while maintaining or improving the level of service to their markets.

The example of a company which has received a great deal of publicity as a leader in this area is the Raytheon Company.[5] The Distributor Products Division of this company introduced a data processing system for automatically replenishing distributor inventories in early 1959. This system involved the inclusion of a prepunched data processing card with each standard package of product shipped to distributors. Distributors, in turn, were instructed to mail these cards to regional ware-

---

[5]This discussion of recent developments at the Raytheon Company depends heavily on a speech by John T. Thompson, general manager, Distributor Products Division, Raytheon Company, at the Distribution Management Association, Inc., in San Francisco, April 13, 1960.

houses on preassigned reorder days for automatic replenishment of items sold during the preceding period. This made it easier and quicker for distributors to place orders, improved their inventory turnover, and made possible lower inventories and improved availability. Also, in 1959 a central warehouse facility was built in Westwood, Massachusetts, and the process of reducing the number of regional warehouses was begun.

Assuming the availability of products at one or more central locations, the place utility of any product can be determined by the amount of time represented in (1) order communication time, (2) order processing time, and (3) transportation time. Raytheon has taken steps to reduce each of these time elements in attempts to reduce inventory requirements and reduce the total cost of physical distribution.

The system of automatic ordering and inventory replenishment making use of prepunched data processing cards reduced the order communication time. At present, the communication order points are regional district offices. Ultimately, data transmitters located in each customer's office will communicate orders directly to central warehouse facilities.

The receipt of orders on punched cards or tapes makes it possible to use computers and other data processing equipment in the processing of orders. As a result, the time required for the processing of orders and the accumulation and packaging of orders is reduced from days to a matter of a few hours.

The compression of transportation time is being accomplished by the use of airfreight. In a prototype demonstration conducted in late 1959, orders were originated in Los Angeles, Chicago, and Dallas and transmitted to the warehouse facility at Westwood. The orders were processed, filled, and shipped by airfreight, reaching their destinations on the same day they were originated. This demonstration proved that the combination of a communications system integrated with an order-processing system and utilization of airfreight can provide improved service to customers with reduced inventory and reduced cost. Raytheon expects to eliminate 50 percent of its dollar investment in inventory. An annual saving of at least $250,000 in direct out-of-pocket expenses is expected to result from their actions.

IMPLICATIONS

Progress in improving the efficiency and reducing the cost of manufacturing and production activities in American business has outstripped similar progress in the area of distribution. Marketing management faces a challenge to bring about similar improvements in distribution activities. Marketing costs, particularly those resulting from the physical distribution of goods, should be given more serious attention if increased productivity is to continue its contribution to increased standards of living. In our economy, those companies which meet this challenge with organizational change and adjustment to new concepts and new tools will have the competitive advantage in the future.

The costs of physical distribution should be considered as an important segment of total marketing costs, worthy of serious analysis and control. There should be an increased awareness that the important physical distribution cost is the total cost of performing these activities. Increased attention should be directed to integration of the subfunctions which comprise physical distribution. Necessary organizational changes should be made to place responsibility for these combined activities at a level which will result in optimization of the integrated whole.

Inventories should be viewed by marketing management as a fundamental element of service to customers. But the accumulation, handling, storing, transportation, and obsolescence of inventories represent substantial costs. Alternative mixes of these inventory cost elements are available for consideration in attempts to maintain or improve service to customers at reduced cost. The location and amount of inventories should be determined in light of the time required for service to customers. Recent developments in reducing the time required for order transmission, order processing, and transportation should be given serious consideration.

Impending improvements in the quality of airfreight service, accompanied by imminent reductions in airfreight rates, represent an opportunity for many companies to improve service to customers with reduced inventory and thus reduce the total cost of performing physical distribution activities. Those companies which make the necessary analyses and adjustments and take advantage of this opportunity will be the leaders in their industries.

6. THE RELATIONSHIP OF TRANSPORTATION TO DISTRIBUTION*

Robert L. Banks

BROADLY, PHYSICAL DISTRIBUTION IS TRANSPORTATION

The title of this paper may make it seem a mere exercise in emphasizing the obvious, for in broad terms, physical distribution is the sum of all the marketing decisions which affect the movement of goods from one place to another. However, the great difference in viewpoint between physical distribution analysis and transportation economics and perhaps the even greater difference in outlook between the individuals engaged in market-

*From *The Social Responsibilities of Marketing*, American Marketing Association, December, 1961, pp. 513-24.

ing or physical distribution management and those with transportation firms merits an examination of the relationship which makes them both participants in an identical economic process.

Physical distribution analysis is system-oriented, it is concerned with the paths of goods moving within the firm and to market, as these movements are a part of its entire production and marketing system. Transportation is the moving portion of the system, it is in fact a combination of the moving portions of many systems, the consolidated flows of goods originating with many firms. Where distribution analysis is concerned with the movement of goods as a part of the producing and marketing process of particular firms, transportation is concerned with many different product lines of many different firms, moving between a multitude of origins and destinations.

In the view of the distribution executive, transportation facilities, whether common carrier or producer-owned and operated, are tools with which costs can be minimized and profit contributions maximized. From the viewpoint of a transportation company, by contrast, distribution managers create the demands which must be satisfied. The proper concern of both users and producers of transportation is to minimize the resources devoted to, that is, the costs of, physical distribution.

PHYSICAL AND ENGINEERING REQUIREMENTS OF THE DISTRIBUTION SYSTEM

An ideal or optimum distribution system would presumably be part of an ideal manufacturing and marketing system. In this utopia all the parts would mesh perfectly together to produce the most efficient results at the lowest possible total cost. Physical distribution would perfectly complement production and sales, and transportation would be the perfect tool of physical distribution. Specifically, factories, warehouses and wholesale and retail establishments would be laid out for efficient materials handling geared to the most advantageous means of intercity transportation. However alluring this prospect, physical distribution in reality must often compromise with inherited facilities and budgetary limitations.

Plants designed by architects or engineers quite conscious of internal processing requirements or of human amenities may reflect inadequate consideration of physical distribution requirements. As a result, the product may suffer from distribution diseconomies which could be, and often are, quite substantial. In other cases, transportation and indeed overall systems savings may require investment in storage space or in materials handling equipment which, while it might pay for itself in the long run, represents a burdensome expense. Alternative choices—always an important strategic consideration—may be narrowed or eliminated because private sidings and wharves are quite expensive to install; in the absence of advance planning their installation may be virtually impossible.

THE INFLUENCE OF NONPHYSICAL FACTORS ON PHYSICAL DISTRIBUTION AND TRANSPORTATION

INDUSTRY PRICING PATTERNS AND COMPETITIVE PRACTICES

If all goods were sold f.o.b. point of production, purchasers would weigh very carefully the rates and services of the various carriers. If quantity discounts on the part of the manufacturers were to supplement low freight rates for large-volume shipments, these incentives would tend more to offset the disadvantages of buying in large quantities. In many cases, however, producers will absorb freight charges so as to compete in distant markets. In such cases, if the receiver or purchaser specifies the means of transportation, convenience is everything, economy nothing.

Industry pricing patterns are not the whole story; competition may put a premium on prompt delivery, packaging, or other factors. The customary order quantity and inventory policy likewise have great effect on attainable transportation economies. Here the decisive question is whether the large inventories are kept by the manufacturer or someone further down the distribution chain.

CARRIER RATE PATTERNS AND COMPETITIVE PRACTICES

Carrier rate patterns and competitive practices, both intermodal and among carriers of the same mode, constitute another very important nonphysical influence on distribution and marketing policy. On the railroads, for example, because so many shipments move over more than one carrier, and because of a history of destructive competition, freight rates are more often the work of freight bureaus (mechanisms peculiar to transportation which set prices free of antitrust restraints) than of individual railroads. Thus, with some exceptions, the railroad freight rate for a given commodity from one point to another is the same regardless of the railroads used. There is no direct, open rate competition between railroads. There is, however, service and rate competition of a different kind. It is market competition involving products of the same type from different origins. Railroads competing from Detroit to Chicago will not cut freight rates in an attempt to get the business one from the other, but a third railroad carrying the same commodity from Minneapolis to Chicago may reduce its freight rate in an endeavor to gain or retain the Chicago market for the producer on its line and thus to gain or retain the movement for itself. Such situations are in large measure responsible for the great complexity of the railroad rate structure. Also contributing to the historical development of the rate structure has been the attempt to set relatively low rates for heavy, bulky, low-value raw materials and relatively high rates for high-valued manufactured goods. This so-called "value of service" approach to the pricing of transportation service all too frequently obscures rather than reflects the engineering and economic realities.

Freight bureaus are not confined to railroads alone, but also set prices for water transportation and for trucking, and the rigidity of the freight bureau rate-making system is to some extent offset by the very active rate competition among the various modes of transportation. This competition is intensified by the fact that a large part of highway freight traffic and most inland waterway freight is not under economic regulation, that is, the government does not, for these unregulated parts of the transportation industry, oversee carrier pricing policy.

THE IMPACT OF PRIVATE TRANSPORT

The availability of unregulated private transportation puts a limit upon the diseconomies which may be caused by the irrationalities of carrier rate patterns and competitive practices. If a distribution manager finds public transportation service inadequate or unrealistically priced, he can buy or lease trucks and perform his own transportation. From an overall economic point of view, this may often be an unfortunate solution, because transportation carried on as an adjunct to some other business is not likely to be as efficient as if it were the main function of the firm. On the other hand, the existence of private transport costs as a rate ceiling and private transport operation as a service standard should force public carriers to provide good service at economically realistic rates.

REGULATORY RESTRAINTS ON OPTIMUM TRANSPORT PERFORMANCE

Intercity freight transportation is a good example of economic specialization. Each producer could, theoretically, buy his own trucks and carry his own goods from one stage of production to another and to their final markets. Transportation firms, however, have developed the facilities and the skill to perform this one function efficiently and by gathering together the goods of many producers they are able to utilize resources devoted to transportation much more efficiently than would be the case if each producer did his own shipping.

The development of the railroad made the transportation specialist's advantage almost overwhelming. These advantages are equally obvious in air and water transportation where equipment costs are substantial. But the ease with which today any business may acquire and operate its own trucks has greatly reduced this advantage.

Thus, the theoretical benefits of economic specialization, as valid in transportation as elsewhere, have been obscured by public policy which encourages firms whose primary interests lie outside the transportation industry, to provide their own transportation free of regulatory restraints. Meanwhile, economic regulation denies to all public carriers that flexibility in price competition which would enable them to compete with the shippers' own transportation facilities. This rigidity lies not merely in the requirements imposed for publication of rates and the delays and impediments by which these can be suspended and investigated; it lies also in the tendency of regulation to perpetuate, indeed to embalm, the frequently uneconomic rate patterns mentioned earlier. And all too often regulation is used by public carriers to their mutual disadvantage as a weapon of intermodal competition.

MODERN TRANSPORTATION MUST RECOGNIZE ITS
PHYSICAL DISTRIBUTION FUNCTION

The very facts that modern technology and public policy facilitate private transportation, and that custom and regulation have tended to mask the economies of specialization in this field only emphasize the imperative necessity for common carriers to exploit their inherent advantages. If the common carrier network as we have known it is to survive and prosper, it must broaden its view of itself. No longer can transportation be regarded as an isolated function, physically and conceptually removed from the production process. Today air, motor, water, and rail carriers are beginning to recognize that their proper role is as part of the total marketing mechanism for the nation's goods. In this posture, realization of their potential requires performance surpassing that which the shipper can provide for himself.

CARRIERS ARE SELLING A SERVICE, COMPETING WITH EACH OTHER,
AND WITH "DO-IT-YOURSELF"

Although freight transportation is intensely competitive, the competitive effort in general is far too narrowly directed. Railroad freight salesmen feel they have achieved great success when they get a few carloads away from another railroad. A truckline is proud of service which enables it to win business away from a parallel railroad, while charging higher rates. Yet the growth of private and unregulated carriage shows that neither the railroad nor the truckline is being truly successful in its competitive efforts. The existence of this blind spot is beginning to be recognized and recognition should be the first step toward a cure. Up to this moment, however, the first step seems typically negative and responsive. It is too often apt to be simply a rate reduction reflecting a shipper's threat to go out and buy his own trucks.

THE SERVICE IS NOT TON-MILES,
AND THE PRICE IS NOT THE FREIGHT RATE

Volume of transportation is measured in ton-miles, and transportation firms frequently think and speak of themselves as manufacturers of ton-miles. More properly they are producing a service. The service that they sell is to provide a part of the distribution system, and its price is controlled by alternative transportation arrangements available to the user. The proper objective of the modern transportation firm should be to move each customer's goods in a manner which minimizes the total cost of manufacturing, storing, transporting, packaging, and marketing. This minimization of total cost is the proper objective because minimal movement cost does not necessarily equate with minimal total cost, and because change in transportation can well induce or require changes in every other part of the marketing process.

Actually, to operate a transportation system on this basis is a very large order indeed. In fact, the transportation firms cannot do it unassisted. No transportation man knows more about the firms he serves than they themselves do, but if a transportation salesman knows intimately the capabilities of his own company, if he really believes that his function is to be a part of a distribution system, and if he has an informed, intelligent understanding of physical distribution, he can work with distribution managers to tailor transportation services to physical distribution requirements. Such men have until now been few, but their number is increasing, as transportation firms have in recent years begun to realize that modern merchandising of their product requires a consumer orientation as long absent in transportation as it has been present in other industries.

NEITHER FASTEST NOR CHEAPEST IS NECESSARILY APPROPRIATE

When emphasis is placed upon such factors as the capital tied up in inventory, one might conclude that the fastest transportation is always the most desirable. Considering only direct expenses, one could by contrast conclude that the least expensive is preferable. Actually, of course, neither fastest nor cheapest transportation is necessarily best suited to particular situations.

Sand is a commodity of low value, easily stored. It can be piled outdoors at no great expense for protection and rehandling. A large amount of it can be in inventory without tying up much capital. Since it is of low value, even a moderate freight rate is fairly large in proportion to the cost of the sand itself. Under these circumstances, it is not surprising that the direct cost of transportation is very important in the movement of sand. The users of sand are quite willing to accept long and irregular travel time and shipment in large quantities in order to get low freight rates.

Transistors are a contrasting case. They are light, compact, extremely expensive and require protection in movement and storage. Few purchasers use transistors in large lots, and to tie up a substantial quantity in storage or slow movement for even a few days would mean freezing significant amounts of working capital. Even the highest freight rate would represent a very small fraction of the price of a transistor. More important considerations are careful, expeditious and dependable movement. Yet even here, the very fastest transportation may not be the wisest choice. Transport arrangements involving a single extra day may not result in prohibitive interest cost if the slightly lower cost transportation gives greater dependability, so that the consumer of transistors need not carry a protective stock.

The true economies of transportation are sometimes paradoxical. In the cases of lumber and coal, for example, the transport and warehousing functions are thoroughly commingled. As a result of operating changes, one railroad was able to reduce the transport time of an important coal movement by a full day. This apparent improvement in service resulted in no increase in freight charges, yet the customers were not pleased; quite the reverse. The expedited movement gave the concerned coal brokers insufficient time to sell their product. The case of lumber is perhaps better known. Since the provision of a storage service in addition to transportation could be considered "undue preference," the Interstate Commerce Commission felt it necessary to issue an order forbidding deliberate delays by rail carriers engaged in transporting lumber, such delays arising from their desire to afford their customers a needed and wanted service.

TRANSPORTATION A PART OF THE SYSTEM

The best type of transportation in each instance cannot be chosen simply by considering the nature of the commodity to be moved. Production and sales quantities also have a very important influence on the optimum transportation design. If the customary lot size of manufacturing runs of orders is large, it lends itself to bulk, normally cheaper, transportation. If the lot sizes are small, the user of transportation may elect to accumulate a considerable manufacturing run and then ship it to a warehouse, where it is again stored until purchased in small quantities. Thus there can be a double storage cost, the elimination of which can justify fairly high freight charges, if the alternative of small-lot frequent shipment direct from producer to consumer or retail outlet is available. But manufacturing is the very inventor of economies of scale; customary lot sizes may well need reviewing. If discounts are offered to reflect economies in manufacture and shipment, purchasers may suddenly find that they can order large quantities after all. The questions of storage and standard quantities are, of course, related. Where the final purchases are necessarily small, mass production and volume transportation may make distribution from several strategically located warehouses very attractive.

Handling and packaging are parts of the transportation cost that do not appear in the freight charges. Shipments by railroad and by ship are apt to require rehandlings which are expensive in themselves, and which together with exposure in movement lead to the necessity for more expensive packaging than is required for truck or air movement. Perhaps the extreme in packaging is that which was said to be required of electronic equipment moving overseas during World War II. This was supposed to be packed so that it could be rolled down a long flight of stairs, dropped three feet onto a concrete platform and subsequently left on the beach at low tide. Even less rigorous packaging requirements may add significant increments to total distribution expense, and in fact be the ultimate determinant of choice among several transport alternatives. Closely related to handling and packaging are problems of loss, damage, and spoilage. Container and piggyback systems, by eliminating intermediate handlings, frequently reduce loss and damage and simplify packaging. Ultimately, such systems, due to these and other advantages, are likely to play an important role in the distribution mechanics of the nation.

A carrier which subjects goods to loss, damage, or spoilage is laboring under a severe handicap. It must offer very substantial economies in freight charges or in other items to offset this disadvantage. The measure of the competitive handicap is not just the amount of damage claims made. Such claims represent the cost to repair or replace the goods involved, but the receiver of freight does not want his goods repaired or replaced at some later date; he wants them in good order when he receives them. The administrative cost of pressing claims and the more serious cost of delay in receiving anticipated shipments will be assessed pretty highly.

We are now able to formulate the general criteria for design of a distribution system, a design which imposes the requirements to be met by modern transportation firms. Such a system must consciously relate the manufacturing and marketing processes of the involved commodities to the points between which they are to move, and the characteristics of the various types of public and private transportation which are available. After analyzing the nature of the production system, the location of the purchasers, the size and frequency of their orders, and established pricing and selling practices, a distribution manager could lay out a movement pattern for a whole variety of commodities between different origins and destinations, in different quantities, with different requirements as to speed, regularity, and other service characteristics. For each of these movements in the pattern, he would determine alternative costs of providing transportation which most nearly fit the pattern requirement. Where direct transportation costs of the initial design appeared high, these could be weighed against costs of providing less expensive types of transportation, adding to these lower transportation charges, the inventory costs of goods in transit and the inventory and storage costs of goods in protective stocks. Alternative designs would be formulated for variations in production volume of each involved commodity. Then the prudent distribution manager would make a searching reexamination of the whole system. Should he combine movements to gain the benefits of quantity? If he is contemplating private transportation can he rearrange his pattern to provide back hauls? Can customary shipping quantities and perhaps other traditional market practices be reconsidered to make possible savings not only in transportation but in manufacture?

Obviously, pat solutions are unlikely. A one-plant manufacturer with a national market could eliminate all local and regional stocks and could ship by air exclusively. Such a system has the virtue of simplicity. The saving from elimination of outlying stocks can be calculated. Presumably, to justify such a system, it would save enough to pay for the airfreight. But airfreight is not the total transport cost. A larger plant storage area; a high-capacity, high-speed inventory control and order system; and possibly a leased-wire network will be required. Even then, some customers may be lost because they can't buy off the shelf. When all these factors are weighed, the system may still be worthwhile. The danger is that they will not be weighed, that lack of appropriate analysis will burden a firm with a modern, fashionable distribution system that increases expenses and reduces sales. In short, the fundamental criterion for the design of a distribution system is that it be considered a part of the total operations of the particular firm and that the design comprehend the most advanced knowledge of every facet of these operations.

CARRIER CHARACTERISTICS AS A FACTOR IN SHIPPER CHOICE

Each form of transportation suffers or enjoys well-known handicaps and advantages. Water transportation can offer low freight charges but at the expense of slow service and necessarily large quantity shipments. Air transportation is well suited to shipment in small quantities and offers great speed but air cargo rates are very high. Rail and truck transportation generally lie between these two extremes. It would be ridiculous for an airline to offer to carry freight at barge rates and it would be equally hopeless for a barge line to attempt to match airline service standards. Unfortunately, the handicaps are not always acknowledged, nor the advantages exploited. Many rail carload freight rates are based upon minimum weights which are equal to a truckload, thus effectively wasting the boxcar's larger capacity. On the other hand there are instances of low truck rates based a two-truckload minimum weight, although the economy of moving two truckloads at once is negligible. Generally, truck and air carriers exploit the service advantages which they frequently enjoy of greater speed, lower minimum weight, less damage, simpler packaging, and greater flexibility. Railroad and water carriers properly exploit their efficiency in producing ton-miles. Railroads, at any rate, could do much more in this line. There needs to be more development of incentive rates to encourage full loading of cars and of multiple carload rates to take advantage of the efficiencies of group or even trainload movements.

On the other hand, some defects should be overcome by service improvement rather than simply offset by lower freight rates. While trucking is not as fast as an airplane, the expense of extra handling and the time consumed going to and from the airport may well enable a truck to compete in speed for movements up to a distance of several hundred miles because generally overnight movement is all that is required. There is no great gain in having goods arrive at 3 A.M. if a plant doesn't open until 7. For journeys of moderate length, the time spent in gathering cars into trains and sorting them out again may well make rail transportation slower than truck, but there appears to be no sound reason why it should also be less dependable.

SPECIAL PROBLEMS OF TRANSPORTATION AS A REGULATED UTILITY

Common carrier transportation companies are regulated like public utilities even though intercarrier and intermodal competition is keen; and all such carriers compete with unregulated and private transportation. This combination of competition and public utility type regulation distinguishes public transportation from other forms of economic activity. Adjustment of rates to change in supply and demand is a slow and difficult process. Of course, stability in freight rates is to some extent desirable to enable businessmen to plan where they can buy and sell and to enable distribution managers to work with some degree of foresight. But nearly complete rigidity creates diseconomies and frequently leads to use of less economical means of transportation or of some less economical alternative to transportation such as excessive decentralization of plants or warehouses.

Regulation is not confined to rates. Highway and air carriers are restricted as to the routes they may follow and the points they may serve. Such restrictions can lengthen hauls, reduce load factors, and limit the ability to serve the public. These restrictions and those imposed upon the entry of new carriers into the field limit competition, but they have arisen in response to very real historical problems. Railroads in the 19th century paradoxically illustrated the evils of both monopoly and destructive competition. As a result, regulation has attempted to serve conflicting objectives. It attempts to substitute for competition, to preserve competition, and to limit the extent of competition under the very different conditions which obtain today. These aims are not only mutually exclusive, they are in many respects outdated.

Another public utility obligation is the duty to serve all comers and generally to continue to give all the services for which the company was originally chartered. The construction contractor has a perfect right to decline to bid on a job which doesn't look attractive to him, but a common carrier must accept any business offered to the limit of its ability, even though changing conditions may have made some phases of its business unprofitable and burdensome to the rest of its operations.

SUMMARY

Physical distribution and transportation are more or less synonymous terms as used by two different disciplines. Those who practice these disciplines should be conscious of this identity of interest and function.

Such a consciousness will help assist executives to set up appropriate distribution systems for their companies, providing their own transportation and using the various types of for-hire transportation, as each may fit their need of system optimization. Managements of transportation firms are beginning to understand their role as functioning parts of the distribution systems of all their customers, they are beginning to cooperate with distribution managers in fulfilling this role and in learning and teaching how they can broaden the contribution they undoubtedly make. While so doing, transportation managers are not overlooking the fundamental economies of public transportation in general and of their own type of transportation in particular. Mutual understanding between the professions of transportation and distribution management will improve the standards of each, will strengthen the system of public transportation, will benefit the users of transportation, and by increasing the efficiency of production and marketing will increase the wealth of society.

7. MILESTONES ON THE ROAD OF PHYSICAL DISTRIBUTION*

Lewis M. Schneider

A recent trend in industry has been for management to think of the movement and stockpiling of raw materials and finished goods as a system; to identify the interfaces, or common boundaries, between decision-making units within this system; and to coordinate decision making within the firm so as to reduce the total costs of materials flow. This activity is popularly known under a variety of names, including materials management, physical distribution, distribution management, or business logistics. For the purposes of this paper, the term physical distribution will be used to denote the planning and administration of raw materials and finished products, necessarily including or coordinating with the functions of raw material procurement, choices of transportation, warehousing, information flows, customer service standards, data processing, inventory control, and production scheduling.

It is clear that none of the above functions is new in and of itself. What has changed is the way in which they are being administered today. Authority and responsibility in many firms now are being delegated for the conscious coordination of physical distribution activity. For the first time "tradeoffs" within the system (for example inventory levels *versus* mode of transportation) are being evaluated realistically with the result that customer service standards can be met at lower physical distribution costs for the firm.

*From *Reflections on Progress in Marketing,* American Marketing Association, 1964, pp. 395–407.

This paper will spotlight briefly some of the highlights in the development of physical distribution administration through use of a simple conceptual framework. The focus will be on the physical distribution activities carried on in industry and the academic world. It will be shown that the increase in such activity has resulted from four major forces: (1) changes in customer demand patterns, (2) economic pressures on industry, (3) technological change and the application of quantitative techniques to business problems, and (4) the developments in military logistics.

It is important to note the interface between industry and the academic community. Industry has benefited from academic research and has recruited college graduates trained in physical distribution skills. On the other hand, the academic world has improved its course offerings and found research opportunities through close contact with physical distribution developments in industry.

Figure 1 shows the interrelationships between the four environmental pressures, industry, and our universities. The remainder of this paper will be devoted to a discussion of each of the elements in the diagram.

FIGURE 1

The Environment of Physical Distribution Development

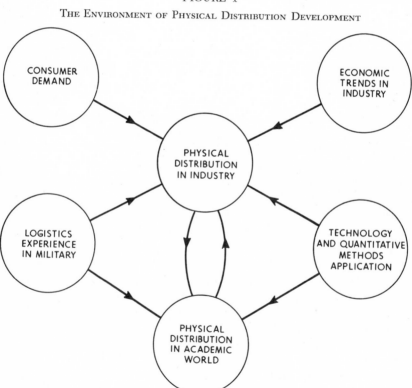

CHANGES IN CONSUMER DEMAND

During the past two decades consumer demands have changed significantly. The aggregate statistics conceal important trends. True, national income data, such as shown in Table 1, indicate that personal consumption expenditures have increased with and maintained almost a constant ratio to the gross national product; that consumption for services has increased relative to nondurables and durables; and that spending on durables dropped during the recession year 1958, but since that time has climbed toward the higher levels of the early 1950's. But these statistics don't show two major problems which have confronted management—product proliferation and locational shifts in consumer purchasing patterns.

TABLE 1

SELECTED STATISTICS—NATIONAL INCOME
PERSONAL CONSUMPTION EXPENDITURES
(all $'s in billions)

Year	Gross National Product	Total	% of GNP	Dur- ables	% of GNP	Non- durables	% of GNP	Ser- vices	% of GNP
1945	...$213.6	$121.7	57.0%	$ 8.1	3.8%	$ 73.2	34.3%	$ 40.4	18.9%
1950	... 284.6	195.0	68.5	30.4	10.7	99.8	35.0	64.9	22.8
1955	... 397.5	256.9	64.6	39.6	10.0	124.8	31.4	92.5	23.2
1958	... 444.5	293.2	66.0	37.3	8.4	141.6	31.9	114.3	25.7
1960	... 503.4	328.2	65.2	44.9	8.9	151.8	30.2	131.5	26.1
1963	... 583.9	375.0	64.2	52.1	8.9	167.5	28.7	155.3	26.6

Source: U.S. Department of Commerce, *Survey of Current Business.*

It is a moot question whether product proliferation has resulted from inherent desire of the consumer to own unique possessions or whether it was a device by which manufacturers were able to achieve product obsolescence (and higher sales) plus price flexibility from "closeouts." It is enough to observe that consumer durables now appear in an infinite variety of colors and styles. The pressures on inventories from the introduction of new product lines has been great. John Magee has found that replacing one line item with three at the same aggregate volume increased inventory requirements 60 percent.[1] Even when the broader three-item product line increased aggregate sales 50 percent, inventory requirements still doubled and the inventory cost per unit sold increased over 30 percent.

---

[1]John F. Magee, "The Logistics of Distribution," *Harvard Business Review,* July–August, 1960, p. 91.

The locational shifts in consumer demands have taken three forms. Nationwide, the growing population has moved from the farms to the cities and from the East and Northeast to the West and Southwest. Within urban areas consumer demands are now met increasingly by the modern suburban shopping center. Retailers which once confined their activity to the core city now have mixed allegiances between central city and suburbia, again with resulting pressures on inventory levels because of multiple stock locations. The growing importance of the West and Southwest have compelled firms to build new plants and warehouses and change their traditional choices of transportation.

In short, physical distribution "dances to the tune" of consumer demand. Because of the shifts in demand patterns, traditional distribution techniques have become increasingly unsatisfactory from a cost and customer service standpoint, and an environment within business has been created in which new techniques and organizational patterns have a greater chance of acceptance.

ECONOMIC PRESSURES ON INDUSTRY

Simultaneously with changing demand patterns, industry has encountered strong upward pressures on labor costs. Often these costs have directly affected the physical distribution function in activities such as warehousing, transportation, and clerical information processing. Rigidities such as a guaranteed work week or supplemental unemployment benefits have transformed variable production costs into semifixed or fixed expenses. Revenues have not kept pace with rising costs. A recent study by the National Industrial Conference Board reported that corporate profits before taxes as a percentage of assets declined from the 10 percent levels of the early postwar years to below 6 percent by the late 1950's. Profits before taxes as compared to the previous year fell sharply in 1952, 1954, 1958, and 1960. Even the increase in profits since 1961 has not brought the return on total assets much above 6 percent.[2]

The profit squeeze has been a major force in the reorganization for physical distribution. As profits declined, corporate managements acted swiftly and in the face of production cost rigidities turned to the often hitherto untouched physical distribution functions for cost reductions. As the physical distribution sector "tightened its budgetary belt" new procedures became the rule rather than the exception. Changes in consumer demands reinforced by the profit squeeze forced the physical distribution problem into the open.

---

[2]"The Economic Environment of the Middle Sixties," *The Conference Board Record I*, September, 1964, p. 30.

TECHNOLOGICAL CHANGE AND THE APPLICATION OF
QUANTITATIVE TECHNIQUES TO BUSINESS

TECHNOLOGICAL CHANGE

Fortunately technological changes during the past decade have helped ease the physical distribution dilemma. These developments will be summarized briefly under the headings of transportation, materials handling and warehousing, communications, and data processing.

Transportation. The net effect of technological change has been to improve transportation service (both public and private) at a lower cost to the nation. In the aggregate, the nation's total freight bill dropped from 9.2 percent of the GNP in 1958 to 8.7 percent in 1962.[3] At the same time transit times have improved in many cases and special equipment has reduced loss and damage claims.

The railroads have completed the conversion from steam to diesel power, rebuilt classification yards, inaugurated piggyback, container and bulk commodity unit train service, and invested in other specialized freight equipment such as high cube boxcars.

The motor carrier industry has invested in equipment with heavier load-carrying capacity, thereby reducing ton-mile costs. The average load carried per truck combination (truck and trailer) rose from about 10½ to 12½ tons between 1950 and 1962.[4] Motor carrier transportation has become increasingly attractive as the $41 billion interstate expressway system moves toward completion.

Water transportation also has benefited from government promotion of transportation facilities (the federal expenditures alone for waterways in 1963 was $314.6 million).[5] The most modern inland waterway diesel-powered tows can produce 4 million ton-miles per day upstream and 10 million ton-miles per day downstream at a cost of less than one-half cent per ton mile.[6]

Perhaps the most dramatic transportation technological development has been the inauguration of turboprop and pure jet freight airplanes. Historically, airfreight traffic growth was greatly hampered by high piston engine airplane operating costs and the resulting high freight

---

[3]Transportation Association of America, *Transportation Facts & Trends* (Washington, D.C., 1964), p. 3. This booklet is an excellent source for data on the transportation industry.

[4]Automobile Manufacturers Association, *Motor Truck Facts 1964* (Detroit, 1964), p. 41.

[5]Association of American Railroads, *Government Expenditures for Construction, Operation, and Maintenance of Transport Facilities by Air, Highway, and Waterway and Private Expenditures for Construction, Maintenance of Way, and Taxes on Railroad Facilities* (Washington, D.C., 1964), p. 9.

[6]For a recent discussion of inland waterway transportation see "Flood Tide for the Barges," *Business Week*, August 1, 1964, p. 48.

rates (typically in excess of 20 cents per ton-mile). The advent of turbo-props and pure jets has slashed ton-mile costs. Recently, it was announced that the 550 m.p.h. C-141 jet freighter could operate profitably at a freight rate of 10 cents per ton-mile with a 60 percent load factor.[7] By comparison, truck rates range from 6–8 cents per ton-mile, on the average. Naturally the dramatic block-to-block speed of air transportation has the potential to reduce inventory pipeline time in a firm's distribution system. The question will be whether the industry can provide fast terminal pickup and delivery schedules and keep rates low enough to generate a high volume of traffic. In 1963 the airlines' share of the domestic ton-miles was only 0.09 percent.

The last elements in the domestic transportation picture are pipelines and conveyor belts. The oil pipelines' share of the nation's ton-miles has remained constant at about 17 percent.[8] Some special-purpose pipelines and conveyor belts for other bulk products are in operation, but a massive replacement of rail or water facilities by pipeline does not seem likely during the next decade. Indeed, the railroads were able to force a coal pipeline to close in 1963 by offering substantially lower unit-trainload rates.

Warehouse administration and materials handling. Warehouse efficiency has been improved through the substitution of capital investments for labor. The new techniques include palletization and containerization to eliminate manual placement (and minimize damage claims), conveyors and gravity feed devices to speed the flow of goods and automated equipment for filling orders. Rather than elaborate on this subject, the author refers the reader to the indicated references.[9]

Communications and data processing. Physical distribution encompasses more than just the physical storage and shipment of goods. The transportation and placement decisions result from the interaction between consumer demand, production schedules, and purchasing policies. Each is linked by communications and data processing.

Again, it would not be appropriate in this paper to trace in depth the technological changes surrounding communications and data processing. In brief, the order processing pipeline has been shortened by the substitution of direct telephone, teletype, or electronic communications networks for the mail. Computers have replaced clerical personnel in the tedious routines of updating, aggregating and reporting information

---

[7]*Aviation Week*, August 24, 1964, p. 45.

[8]For statistics showing ton-miles distributed by mode of transportation see Interstate Commerce Commission, *Transport Economics.*

[9]See James R. Bright, *Management Guide to Productivity* (Yale & Towne Manufacturing Co., 1961); Joseph E. Wiltrakis, *The Automatic Warehouse—Key to Distribution* (Western Electric Co., 1962); and a list of suggested readings in J. L. Heskett, Robert M. Ivie, and Nicholas A. Glaskowsky, Jr., *Business Logistics* (New York: The Ronald Press, 1964), p. 414.

on sales, inventories, shipments, etc. In many cases decision rules are programmed into the integrated computer systems in the effort to reduce the possibility of poor decisions at lower levels of management. For example, an integrated computer system can record sales by line item and initiate a replenishment order for a given quantity when a "trigger point" is reached, thereby replacing an inventory clerk with a Kardex file.

Of course, there can be (and frequently are) disconcerting problems associated with changing from manual to computerized systems. One documented study of electronic data processing published at Harvard Business School pointed out the increased costs and less-than-hoped-for benefits resulting from computers in certain situations.[10] On the other hand, the shifts from small local warehouses to larger regional distribution warehouses, continual product proliferation, pressure to improve customer service, and the rising clerical costs of manual data processing will probably result in the expansion of improved communication and data processing capabilities within physical distribution.

QUANTITATIVE TECHNIQUES

Hand in hand with the computers have come more sophisticated approaches to analyzing and solving business problems. The physical distribution area has been a "natural subject" for research and the application of quantitative techniques. Mathematical programming models have been formulated to yield inventory reorder point and reorder quantity decision rules; determine optimal warehouse and plant locations; determine which plants should fill customer or warehouse orders; choose modes of transportation; and even compute the size of a loading dock to reduce vehicle waiting time.[11]

The operations research technician has appeared on the scene complete with a "bag of tools" including regression analysis, exponential smoothing, linear programming, dynamic programming, waiting line theory, etc. His presence has not always been welcomed, for many practitioners within the industrial physical distribution community have relied on "tried and true" tested remedies for their problems and view the mathematical models, Fortran programs, and computer print-outs with suspicion and distrust. (This holds true for the academic community as well.)

Yet, as the application of mathematical techniques improves management decision making, it will gain acceptance. Already the lines of communication are beginning to become more friendly between the old-time practitioner and the newly arrived staff specialist.

[10]John P. McNerney, *Installing and Using an Automatic Data Processing System* (Boston: Harvard Business School Division of Research, 1961), pp. 286–87.

[11]For lists of suggested readings of varying mathematical difficulty on applications of quantitative techniques to physical distribution see Heskett *et al., op. cit.,* pp. 341 and 375.

The military experience

As noted, physical distribution is often known under the name "business logistics." Logistics was originally a military term, defined by Webster as "that branch of the military art which embraces the details of the transport, quartering, and supply of troops." Military logistics differs from industrial physical distribution in several respects.

The objective function of the military is to win wars rather than generate an adequate return on investment, thus its imputed costs of stock-out could exceed greatly that of industry. Second, a major military logistics problem is the movement and provisioning of personnel, whereas industrial physical distribution concentrates primarily on materials flows. Third, in the military a substantial amount of logistics activities involves maintenance and modification of equipment. In industry, maintenance and modification are the responsibility of the production organization.

Following the Korean War all branches of the military began to reevaluate their logistic policies in large part because of the excesses of inventory being generated by the development of new weapons systems. Substantial changes in inventory, warehouse location, and transportation policies resulted. For example, the Air Force Logistics Command turned to air transportation between its major depots and base supply warehouses in order to reduce field inventories. By 1962 the Air Force was moving 12 percent of its tonnage (the equivalent of 12,000 freight cars) by its Logair system.[12]

Clearly the military's logistics problems are massive. In 1962 the spare parts inventory of the Air Force Logistics Command was valued at $12.2 billion, purchases for inventory totaled $3.3 billion, and employment was 148,000 persons. The Air Force (as well as the other services) has made great strides in establishing computerized priority systems of inventory control, automated warehouses, single-point inventory management, and containerization.

The military has also sponsored basic and applied operations research on logistics problems. One recent study for the Air Force applies the latest theories of Bayesian statistical decision making to a simulation of inventory reordering policies.[13]

In short the military logistics experience has provided industry with a sort of immense proving ground for research and application of physical distribution techniques. It seems quite possible that the changes in

---

[12]The descriptive material on the Air Force Logistics Command is contained in Air Force Logistics Command, "Presentation on Logistics Management," September 7, 1963 (mimeographed).

[13]G. J. Feeney, J. W. Petersen, and C. C. Sherbrooke, *An Aggregate Base Stockage Policy for Recoverable Spare Parts* (Santa Monica: The RAND Corporation, 1963). See also J. W. Petersen, H. W. Nelson, and R. M. Paulson, *The Costs and Benefits of Responsive Support Operations* (Santa Monica: The RAND Corporation, 1962).

industry might have come more slowly had it not been for the military experience.

PHYSICAL DISTRIBUTION IN INDUSTRY

THE COMPANY LEVEL

The changes in organization and techniques for physical distribution within industry have been documented by recent surveys made by *Transportation & Distribution Management* magazine. Their 1963 survey of 219 companies found that 44 percent had created distribution departments for integrated physical distribution management.[14] These departments primarily integrated the functions of transportation, warehousing, order processing, and plant and warehouse location, and to a lesser extent were responsible for inventory control, material handling, protective packaging, production planning, and market forecasting (Table 2). Although it is difficult to determine whether the new distribution departments had formal responsibility or simply "actively participated in" the above functions, it is clear that groups which once were concerned only with traffic and transportation have now branched out into other areas of the logistics system.

TABLE 2

FUNCTIONAL RESPONSIBILITIES OF DISTRIBUTION DEPARTMENTS

Function	Percent of Distribution Departments Having This Function as a Primary Responsibility
Transportation and traffic	85.7%
Warehousing	82.7
Order processing	66.3
Plant and warehouse location	64.3
Material handling (nonproduction line)	57.1
Inventory control	57.1
Protective packaging	42.9
Production planning	30.6
Market forecasting	21.4

Source: *Transportation and Distribution Management* (October, 1963).

Their survey also spotlighted the more common fragmentation of the physical distribution function, for in the remaining 56 percent of the companies responsibility was divided among the plant manager, warehouse manager, traffic manager, chief engineer, production manager, sales manager, order department manager, purchasing agent, market research manager, and president (Table 3).

---

[14]"Physical Distribution Management: How It Is Organized," *Transportation and Distribution Management III*, October and November, 1963.

TABLE 3

BREAKDOWN OF FUNCTIONAL RESPONSIBILITIES
NONDISTRIBUTION DEPARTMENT COMPANIES

Function	Principal Managers of This Activity and Incidence of Response
Traffic and Transportation	Traffic manager 84.4%
Warehousing	Traffic manager 31.9%, warehouse manager 19.2%, production manager 8.1%
Order processing	Order department manager, 18.5%, sales manager 17.7%, traffic manager 13.2%
Plant and wholesale location ...	Traffic manager 24.0%, sales manager 9.7%, president 8.3%
Material handling	Plant manager, 12.2%, production manager 16.6%, traffic manager 14.9%
Inventory control	Production manager 38.2%, purchasing agent 10.0%, traffic manager 9.0%
Protective packaging	Traffic manager 18.0%, production manager 12.3%, chief engineer 11.4%
Production planning	Production manager 57.7%, plant manager 14.6%
Market forecasting	Sales manager 60.0%, market research manager 9.1%

Source: *Transportation and Distribution Management* (November, 1963).

It is apparent that there has been and will continue to be spirited competition within industry to see which official becomes the administrative head of the expanded distribution departments. Sales and production executives want responsibility for physical distribution planning citing their experience in the areas of sales analysis, production planning, and inventory control. At the same time spokesmen for traffic managers are encouraging their group to aspire to higher positions of distribution management because they assert that the traffic manager is intimately familiar with the problems of transportation and warehousing—key components of the logistics network.

TRADE ASSOCIATIONS

Interest in physical distribution at the company level prompted the American Management Association to offer special conferences on physical distribution in October, 1959, and April, 1960. The AMA published the papers presented at these sessions under the title *Management of the Physical Distribution Function*. The booklet included case studies of physical distribution management at Burroughs, Westinghouse, Pillsbury, Federal Pacific Electric, Whirlpool, and Raytheon.[15]

In December, 1963, the National Council of Physical Distribution Management was established to encourage the self-development of skills by its members and to increase recognition by top management of the

---

[15]American Management Association, *Management of the Physical Distribution Function* (New York: American Management Association, 1960).

importance of the physical distribution function. The American Society of Traffic and Transportation is another new group which is promoting better transportation and logistics management.

TRADE JOURNALS AND PERIODICALS

In 1960–61 two periodicals, *Traffic Management* and *Transportation & Distribution Management,* were initiated to serve physical distribution administrators. These magazines feature case studies of companies which have implemented physical distribution departments, surveys of physical distribution activity, and technical articles on mathematical techniques. Other magazines such as *Business Week, Traffic World, Handling and Shipping,* and *Distribution Age* have expanded their treatment of the integrated functional aspects of physical distribution. The latter publication has published annual cost surveys to serve as rough industry guidelines for physical distribution administrators.[16]

As industry continues to search for methods to reduce the total cost of physical distribution, trade association and periodical activity has increased. The problems of physical distribution analysis and implementation are common to all firms; thus it is only natural that formal methods to promote the interchange of ideas should be accelerated.

PHYSICAL DISTRIBUTION IN THE ACADEMIC COMMUNITY

COURSES AND TEXTBOOKS

As might be expected the growth of physical distribution management in industry has produced a demand for skilled personnel. Although many new slots are being filled with experienced men from within the organizations, recruiting for college graduates has begun. The initial courses in physical distribution were developed at Michigan State University. At the present time courses in physical distribution or business logistics are being offered in many schools including Ohio State, Michigan, Harvard Business School, and Stanford. For the past two years, Stanford has sponsored a Business Logistics Forum bringing together academicians and representatives of industry.

Three new textbooks have appeared within the past four years, and older textbooks have been revised to include an emphasis on integrated decision making for physical distribution.[17] It is interesting to note that the newest textbook requires mathematical skills not usually associated with traffic management or warehousing texts. The subjects include linear programming, waiting-line theory, probabilistic models for inventory control, and network theory.

---

[16]See Richard E. Snyder, "Physical Distribution Costs," *Distribution Age,* December, 1963, p. 35.

[17]The new books include Dean S. Ammer, *Materials Management* (Homewood, Ill.: Richard D. Irwin, Inc., 1962); Edward W. Smykay, Donald J. Bowersox, and Frank H. Mossman, *Physical Distribution Management* (New York: Macmillan, 1961); and Heskett *et al., op. cit.*

RESEARCH

Although research efforts cannot be categorized as extensive at the academic level (in contrast to the military or industry), results of faculty and student projects have been published in the aforementioned trade journals, academic journals such as the *Harvard Business Review,* or in book form.

One of the first monographs on the trace-off potential of physical distribution was the *Role of Air Freight in Physical Distribution,* published in 1956 by Harvard Business School.[18] The study found that the abandonment of branch warehouses in favor of a centralized facility plus revamped inventory reorder point and reorder quantity policies and the use of airfreight could reduce dramatically the total costs of physical distribution. On the other hand, the book stressed that the technological innovation of airfreight simply served as the trigger for reevaluation of the inventory and warehouse policies. Much of the savings could have been achieved through better inventory control rules using the existing motor carrier and rail freight forwarder transportation.

Another major research work which has become a text is Jay Forrester's *Industrial Dynamics.*[19] His model of the firm includes materials as one of six flows, and the simulation offers tremendous insight into the problems of inventory and production fluctuations resulting from multiple warehouse levels and the failure to use smoothing techniques.

It can be expected that physical distribution research will increase as universities expand their graduate programs to include physical distribution as an area of specialization.

Research findings and the interchange of ideas at the academic level have been promoted further by association meetings such as the present one. Another group, newly formed, active in physical distribution activities, has been the Transportation Research Forum. Their annual proceedings have included papers on optimum route analysis, logistics simulation games, macroeconomic cost of physical distribution, analysis of customer service standards, and the relationships between incentive transportation rates and inventory levels.[20]

SUMMARY AND CONCLUSIONS

In summary, a new activity has arisen at the industrial and academic levels, under a variety of labels, designed to teach and implement meth-

[18]Howard T. Lewis, James W. Culliton, and Jack D. Steele, *The Role of Air Freight in Physical Distribution* (Boston, Mass.: Harvard Business School Division of Research, 1956).

[19]Jay W. Forrester, *Industrial Dynamics* (Cambridge, Mass.: MIT Press, 1961) (student's edition).

[20]See Transportation Research Forum, *Papers, Third Annual Meeting* (Oxford: Richard B. Cross, 1962) and *Papers, Fourth Annual Meeting* (Oxford: Richard B. Cross, 1963). (The Forum was known as the American Transportation Research Forum prior to 1963.)

ods of planning and controlling the flow of materials through the firm at minimal cost, yet meeting customer standards. The impetus behind the growth of physical distribution has been the changing nature of consumer demand, the profit squeeze on industry, technological change and analytical techniques which have made new procurement and distribution patterns feasible, and the experience of implementing new logistics techniques in the military.

In industry physical distribution has resulted in changed organizational structures and techniques, new associations and publications and additional areas of concern for existing associations and trade journals. Similarly, in the academic world, the new trend toward physical distribution administration has produced new courses, research, and associations.

In a sense physical distribution (or logistics management) is new, yet the individual activities comprising the integrated function are as old as the emergence of modern commercial enterprise. It would not be inappropriate to point out in closing that much the same was true for the concept of marketing when it was first introduced.

Suggested additional AMA readings

Blanding, Warren. "Organizational Structures for Effective Distribution Programming Case Studies," in *Marketing Precision and Executive Action,* pp. 473–82. Chicago: American Marketing Association, 1962.

Evans, Henry K. "A Vast New Storehouse of Transportation and Marketing Data," *Journal of Marketing,* January, 1966, pp. 33–40.

Gunther, Edgar, and Goldstein, Frederick A. *Current Sources of Marketing Information.* Chicago: American Marketing Association, 1960.

Heskett, J. L. "Education for Logistics: A Look to the Future," in *Reflections on Progress in Marketing,* pp. 681–87. Chicago: American Marketing Association, 1964.

————. "A Missing Link in Physical Distribution System Design," *Journal of Marketing,* October, 1966, pp. 37–41.

————. "Ferment in Marketing's Oldest Area," *Journal of Marketing,* October, 1962, pp. 40–45.

Marks, Norton E., and Taylor, Robert M. *Physicial Distribution and Marketing Logistics.* Chicago: American Marketing Association, 1967.

Shutes, George E. "Airfreight from a Marketing Viewpoint," *Journal of Marketing,* October, 1960, pp. 39–43.

Warshaw, Martin R. "Introducing a New Course in Marketing Logistics and Physical Distribution Management," in *Reflections on Progress in Marketing,* pp. 675–80. Chicago: American Marketing Association, 1964.

Part II

LOGISTICS SYSTEMS ANALYSIS

In the logistics operations of a firm, the largest expense is usually incurred in storing and moving goods. The principal investment and a key attribute of physical distribution, however, is the inventory of goods themselves. Current inventory management theory recognizes the elements of order cost, carrying cost, and out-of-stock cost. In a logistics system, these costs must be traded off with transportation costs and customer service. This tradeoff process, by its nature, is a dynamic one, since the distribution requirements are constantly subject to change.

Magee (8) in "Quantitative Analysis of Physical Distribution Systems" discusses the tradeoff requirements of logistics systems and suggests several quantitative methods of selecting optimum systems alternatives. Kuehn (9) in "Logistics of Physical Facilities in Distribution" presents a quantitative approach to warehouse location using a heuristic or self-improving computer-based analysis. Uses of this approach deal with such decision variables as local truck routing and scheduling, demand variability, and truck capacity. Bowersox (10) in "Forces Influencing Finished Inventory Distribution" presents the environmental and managerial forces which have a direct bearing on inventory distribution. He approaches his discussion from the viewpoint of the marketing needs of the firm. Doherty (11) in "A Closer Look at Operations Research" illustrates several quantitative analysis techniques which are useful in studying business logistics processes. He shows the oldest and best known tradeoff in logistics where the cost of ordering and carrying inventory is optimized. Design of a shipment schedule and a sales forecasting model is also shown. Forrester (12) in "Modeling of Market and Company Interactions" examines the dynamic relationship between distribution system elements and illustrates how a combination of factors influences the linkage between a firm's production and the needs of the market it serves. The dynamics of forward promotion and product flow and counterflows of information are discussed.

Finally, Kuehn and Day (13) discuss the dynamic influence of maintaining a constant inventory to sales ratio in a distribution network. The interactive effect of changes in demand and inventory requirements is demonstrated, and the value of accurate forecasts under these conditions is noted.

8. QUANTITATIVE ANALYSIS OF PHYSICAL DISTRIBUTION SYSTEMS*

John F. Magee

THE SYSTEM

I wish to characterize a physical distribution system schematically. The flow of material and information is illustrated in simplified form by Figure 1. Figure 1 shows how a distribution system is made up of a series of inventory or stock points linked by operations. The stock points may in part be under the same roof—for example, inventories of material in varying stages of completion; the corresponding operations may be manufacturing operations—conversion of items withdrawn from one stock point into new items in another stock point.

FIGURE 1

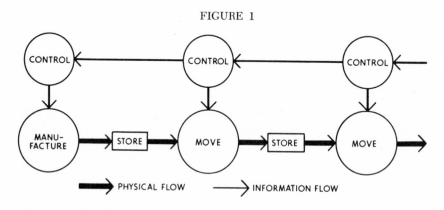

The stock points may also be separated by considerable distances, for example, central plant and field warehouses stocking finished goods. Here transportation is the operation separating individual stock points. Transportation in a field distribution system is much like a manufacturing operation inside a plant. In either case, material is taken out of one stock location and put into another in a different form. Transporting an item

*From *The Social Responsibilities of Marketing*, American Marketing Association, Winter, 1961, pp. 498–512.

changes it, though perhaps not so strikingly as running it through a manufacturing process. After all, a radio tube in a Chicago warehouse is quite a different item in terms of its utility to customers than a tube of the same specifications in Dallas.

The physical product flow—operations transforming items in one stock location into those in another—is governed by a corresponding information flow, in the opposite direction. Customer or user orders place demands on the last stock-keeping stage. This stage, in turn, must follow some procedure to initiate the replenishment operation. This operation in turn draws on the preceding stock unit for the required material.

This highly simplified display of the interrelationship among stock-keeping units, operations, and information processing for an individual item can, in one's imagination, be compounded to represent the highly complex patterns of physical distribution, of material and information flow, which exist in the world today. These complexities arise in part from needs imposed by complex product lines, in part from efforts to balance production, transportation, and marketing effectiveness, in part from regulation.

THE ROLE OF QUANTITATIVE ANALYSIS

Quantitative analysis has a significant role to play in the design of physical distribution systems, first, because the proper choice of a physical distribution plan in the circumstances of any particular company depends not merely on theory or generalizations but on facts, significantly on quantitative facts: costs, times, characteristics of the market and customers, product line characteristics, statisics of demand.

In the second place, physical distribution decisions require a reconciliation or balancing of partly conflicting objectives of a business: low production cost, even flow of product, low transportation paperwork costs, prompt response to market needs:

The production man would like to operate under a level work load with long product runs and minimum disruption. The salesman would like to take selling and promotional action with the comforting knowledge that any demand he might generate would be met, on the spot and without delay. The treasurer would like to keep to a minimum the use of funds to finance plant capacity, inventories, warehouses, and equipment. And so forth.

This balancing act poses difficulties for businesses whose thinking and organization often emphasize traditional functions. For physical distribution is a process in which no function has a dominant interest. Quantitative analysis can help businesses work out the balance among objectives and interests in physical distribution.

I will illustrate that quantitative analysis in physical distribution implies observation and analysis of facts, not merely use of mathematical technique. Physical distribution systems are so complex that there is no single elegant technique for organizing all aspects of a physical distribution study. However, theoretical studies in the last decade have contributed greatly to conceptual understanding and technical apparatus available for studies.

SOME ISSUES AND APPROACHES

Here are some of the significant issues to which quantitative studies can make a contribution:

INVENTORY INVESTMENT

How much should be invested in inventory of a particular item at a given location? I do not propose to go into this question in detail, since it has been covered extensively elsewhere.[1] It is sufficient to note (Figure 2) that one element of the inventory investment (cycle stock) depends on the size of replenishment shipment—a balance of order handling and shipping costs against the cost of holding stock, including the cost of capital. Another element of the inventory investment (safety stock) depends on policies with respect to capital investment and reliability of service, and on the variability of demand, the size of error characteristic of the inventory control forecasts.

The period over which the forecast error or demand variability must

FIGURE 2

CHARACTERISTIC DISTRIBUTION INVENTORY PATTERN

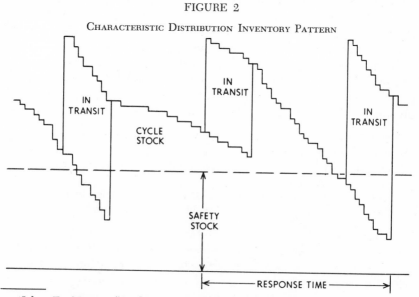

[1]John F. Magee, "Guides to Inventory Policy," *Harvard Business Review,* January–February, March–April, and May–June, 1956.

be measured is the response time or lead time of the replenishment system. Consider, for example, a field warehouse. Its lead time is the time needed for it to make a replenishment order, time to process the order, communications time to the source of supply, perhaps the factory, time for the supply source to make up and load the order, time in transit, plus the fixed time interval, if any, between replenishment orders. For example, if the warehouse is on a biweekly reporting or reordering cycle, the two weeks must be added to the time for paperwork, communications, and transportation.

Quantitative analysis of inventory control systems has contributed substantially 1) in the identification of the system characteristics and costs that must be measured and the policies that must be made explicit, and 2) in the use of inventory control theory to set up means for analyzing demand and making routine replenishment decisions automatically, consistent with policies.

There are clearly interactions between the two elements of inventory I have mentioned. For example, we may lengthen the review period in a field warehouse to cut paperwork and increase the size of replenishment orders for transportation economy. This may, for example, permit shipment in carload lots and carload rates; lengthening the review cycle, however, lengthens the time period over which demand must be forecast and characteristically increases the inventory investment needed to protect order service. However, this is not the time to go into such points in detail. I have introduced the inventory control problem to note that inventory control theory is fundamental to physical distribution studies and to point out the relationship between the inventory investment and the response time or lead time and the time elements that make it up.

CHANGING THE LEAD TIME

I have identified the principal elements of response or lead time as reorder period, processing time, communications time, assembly and loading time, and transportation time. (See Figure 3.) I have also indicated in Figure 3 some of the ways in which the various elements may be speeded up—usually at a cost. For example, we can reorder or report sales from a field warehouse more frequently, daily instead of biweekly; and in the extreme, by customer order. We can use mail, airmail, teletype, or a high-speed data channel like microwave or AT&T's TELPAK. Assembly and loading time may be cut by material handling aids, unitized handling, or possibly mechanized computer-controlled warehousing. You are familiar, I am sure, with the alternatives in transportation and the time and cost characteristics of these. It is noteworthy how many new technical developments can be brought to bear on the physical distribution process, how each new possibility if treated in isolation will tend to increase the cost of the system, how important it is to analyze the characteristics of each new alternative in the light of the response system as a whole.

FIGURE 3

LEAD-TIME COMPONENTS AND SOME REDUCTION POSSIBILITIES

Lead-Time Element	*Reduction Possibilities*
Reorder period	More frequent reorder
	Transmittal of demand order-by-order
Processing time	EDP bookkeeping
	Routine decision rules, using computers
	Real-time processing
Communications time	Teletypewriter
	High-capacity data channels
Material handling time	Unitized handling
	Automatic warehousing
Transportation time	Direct door-door handling
	Air shipment

Analysis is necessary to measure the time characteristics and costs of the available alternatives, to determine what the relationship is, among

FIGURE 4

DEMAND VARIATION V. TIME

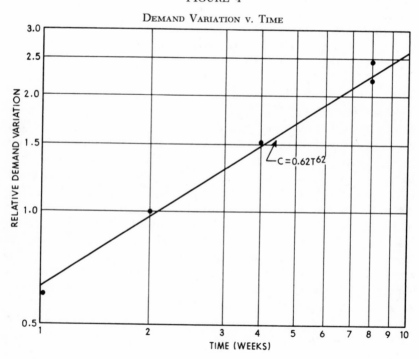

$C = 0.62T^{.62}$

well-balanced alternatives, between response time and system operating cost.

A significant advantage of response or lead-time reduction is reduction in required inventory. I have already noted how inventory investment, at a given service level, depends on demand variability over the lead time. This variability depends, in turn, on the length of the lead time. For example, Figure 4 shows the observed relationship between lead time and relative size of demand variability for one particular product line. It conforms to the general form of relationship we have observed:

$$\sigma_{s,t} = At\alpha \tag{1}$$

where $\sigma_{s,t}$ is the standard deviation of demand v. forecast, observed over time t.

The data in Figure 4 yield a value for α of .62. In some theoretical work, a value of α is arbitrarily assumed, sometimes $\alpha = .5$, sometimes $\alpha = 1.0$. In any real investigation, analysis is necessary to estimate the functional dependence of demand variability on lead time, and if it corresponds to (1), to estimate the value of A and α.

Figure 5 illustrates the balance required between operating cost of the response system and inventory investment. As the lead time increases, operating cost may be reduced (curve A) while the cost of supporting inventory investment increases (curve B), leading to an operating point with minimum total cost (curve C). Since the position of curve B de-

FIGURE 5

ILLUSTRATIVE EFFECT OF LEAD TIME ON TOTAL
DISTRIBUTION SYSTEM COST

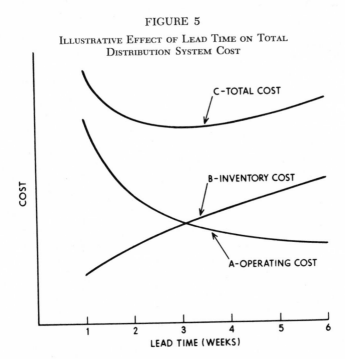

pends on the cost of capital assessed against inventories and on service policies, the minimum-cost operating method is clearly dependent on managerial policy. Quantitative analysis is necessary to measure and state this dependence and to indicate the consequences of policy change.

Both operating costs and investment affected by the replenishment time will depend on the number of points being replenished.

THE NUMBER OF FIELD WAREHOUSES

The minimum number of distribution points—plants, terminals and warehouses from which product is distributed to a customer—will depend on the geographical distribution of product, the acceptable time to deliver an order to a customer, the percentage of the market to be reached in a given time, and the speed of transportation from distribution point to a customer. For example, Table 1 shows the result of a study of the percentage of the U.S. consumer market that can now be reached by truck in a given time from receipt of order at the stated number of distribution points.

TABLE 1

SHARE OF CONSUMER MARKET REACHED, COMPARED WITH TIME
TO REACH, NUMBER OF DISTRIBUTING POINTS

Time	Distribution Points			
	5	25	50	100
1 day	33%	90%	95%	99%
2 days	85	99	100	100

These figures have obviously been affected by improvements in transportation techniques and facilities. Many firms, however, are operating distribution systems designed 20–30 years ago, which do not take advantage of recent major advances in transportation, for example improvement of trucks and road systems.

The table of market service v. time and number of distribution points must be worked out for the particular product line, taking into account its particular market structure. For example, in one case we have found demand roughly proportional to population concentration, with 18 states accounting for 70 percent of demand. In another case, we found demand highly concentrated on the West Coast and in a belt from the Great Lakes east, with 73 percent of demand concentrated in 10 states. Analysis of the pattern and anticipated pattern of demand is critical in distribution system design.

Subject to restrictions on service (and also, to test the price of changing these restrictions), analysis is needed to investigate the economic effects of varying the number of field distribution points. The principal cost elements of concern are:

1. Facilities cost: We generally find the operating cost of a warehouse, including data processing and communication cost, as a function of its normal or design size, to be approximated by

$$C = a + bX$$

and thus, warehousing cost for the system,

$$C_W = aN + bS \qquad (2)$$

where N is the number of warehouses and S is demand in total.

2. Transportation cost: Within a given mode of transport, transportation cost from plant to field distribution point may be affected only in a minor way by the number of distribution points. Outbound transportation from distribution point to customer may follow the form

$$C_{TO} = kN^{-\beta} \qquad (3)$$

where N is the number of warehouses and β depends on the uniformity of market density. (If the market were perfectly uniformly distributed, β would equal .5.)

3. Inventory cost: When distribution point territories are combined, demand variability and thus inventory requirements combine in a complex way. The exact pattern is dependent on the cross-correlation of demand among areas. In practice we find that the variability of demand over a given time interval, as a function of "area" or average demand rate, can be represented as

$$\sigma_{s,d} = gD\alpha \qquad (4)$$

where D is the total average demand and α may generally take on values between .6 and .9.

Clearly, the costs will depend on the modes of operation—for example, degree of warehouse mechanization, type of transportation used, type of communication and data processing system, etc. Thus, the cost balance and economy of operating more or fewer distribution points must be studied in relation to the replenishment system used.

Even at this level of complexity, in the physical distribution study, it is clear that we are dealing with a host of alternatives: in policies— for example, policies with respect to capital cost, service standards; in operating modes—for example, transportation medium, communication and data processing technique; and in extensiveness—for example, the number of distribution points. These alternatives interact; service standards affect relative economy of operating modes, the choice of operating mode influences the cost of expanding or contracting the number of distribution outlets. This condition cries for quantitative analysis to explore these alternatives, subject to the particular statistical characteristics of the market and cost characteristics of the business.

FIGURE 6

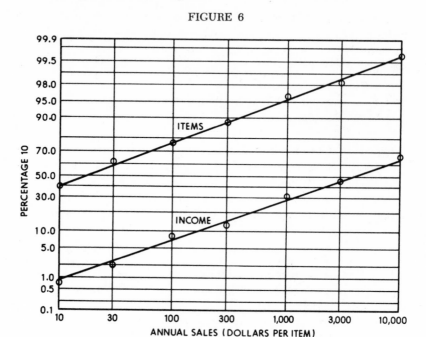

IMPACT OF THE PRODUCT LINE

So far, we have considered physical distribution alternatives as if we are dealing with a single item while at the same time we are examining alternatives for distribution of the product line as a whole. In most businesses, however, we find a product line in which demand is highly concentrated in a few items while most items account for only a modest proportion of sales (Figure 6). The top curve in Figure 6 indicates the fraction of total items (vertical axis) with annual sales equal to or less than the amount shown on the horizontal scale. The lower curve indicates the fraction of total demand indicated by these items. We find this pattern, the lognormal distribution, to be characteristic of most product lines, though the slope (the standard ratio) may vary. This product demand distribution leads to the relationship shown in Figure 7, which illustrates the characteristically high degree of concentration of demand among a small percent of the items in the line.

Other significant characteristics of the product line will also show wide differences. For example, we usually find that inventory requirements increase as the .7–.9 power of average demand. Thus the cost balance underlying the choice of system will depend on the level of demand of the item in question. Figure 8 illustrates some of the alternatives available; we may use programming methods such as the transportation and trans-

FIGURE 7

FRACTION OF TOTAL SALES ACCOUNTED FOR BY FRACTION OF TOTAL ITEMS

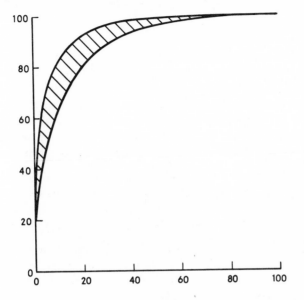

FIGURE 8

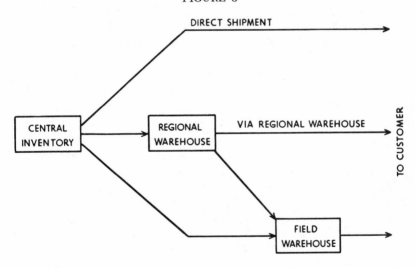

shipment models[2] to study alternate routings for items in the product line, and to define the breakpoints, or conditions which define the bound-

[2]James C. Hetrick, "Mathematical Models in Capital Budgeting," *Harvard Business Review*, January–February, 1961, Appendix, pp. 58 ff.

ary between those items to be distributed one way, for example, direct plant-to-customer, and those to be handled another, for example, stocked in regional warehouses.

PLANNING FOR THE FUTURE

So far I have discussed the problems of distribution systems planning as if the planning were static, as if we could make our plans to meet a static (and presumably well-known) market requirement. In many cases, this is a reasonable assumption; the anticipated rate of change of the market is low enough and the ability to modify the distribution system great enough so that a static view is useful. In many other circumstances, however, we must take a dynamic view of the distribution system:

1. Because change in the system may be expensive and laborious,
2. Because anticipated future needs may be inconsistent with present needs,
3. Because we may not be able to see the future too clearly.

Under these circumstances we may want to give up some immediate advantage in order to be in a better position either to have a system better suited to the future as we anticipate it, without expensive changes, or to be in a more flexible position to deal with the future as it unfolds.

In these problems quantitative analysis can be of great value in working out the consequences of alternative systems under various possible market conditions, a series of static solutions under alternative conditions hypothesized for various future points in time. Our concepts and techniques are still weak, however, for evaluating the consequences of these alternatives with respect to immediate moves.

Let me try to use an illustration to make the problem more explicit. The illustration is taken from Hetrick, although the analysis is not identical. He states the problem as:

A problem arose because of the existence of a manufacturing plant which, although physically adequate, was technologically obsolete and unable to supply the quality of products required in today's market. The plant in question was rather small compared to those then being built. Since it was argued that a plant of this size was at an inherent disadvantage for economic operation, there was considerable managerial controversy over the proper course of action—whether to modernize the operation by construction of better facilities or to scrap the existing plant and supply the area involved from facilities elsewhere, e.g., plants in adjacent states.[3]

Hetrick notes that when the problem was studied using the transportation model of linear programming, under conditions anticipated in the near future, and 5 and 10 years hence, the following pattern of solutions arose (Figure 9).

---

[3]James C. Hetrick, *op. cit.*

FIGURE 9

Program	Near Future	5 Yrs. Hence	10 Yrs. Hence
A. Modernize plant in question Expand elsewhere	"Optimum"		
B. Close plant in question Expand elsewhere		"Optimum"	
C. Modernize and expand the plant in question			"Optimum"

The table shows, for example, that program A gives an optimum balance of operating cost and investment, under the conditions anticipated in the near future, while C is optimum under the conditions anticipated ten years hence. In theory there are 27 plans over time that might be considered, although in practice some are excluded. For example, it was concluded that if program B were adopted, it would be impractical to go to A or C, reopening the plant in question.

There are 11 program sequences that are reasonable, each with its own pattern of investment and operating cost. (In addition there are conceivably other possibilities, represented by solutions intermediate to programs A and C.) On the assumption that conditions in future years are well known, these patterns of investment and operating cost may be evaluated, perhaps by discounted cash flow or present value techniques, although these are not entirely satisfactory.

The situation becomes considerably more difficult, however, if we are seriously uncertain about the market or costs five to ten years hence. Then, though the number of alternative programs may not increase, the evaluation of these alternatives becomes difficult. This is not simply a matter of computational volume, but of conceptual fuzziness. The value of flexibility, the value of avoiding current commitments where there is a significant element of risk due to inflexibility, becomes high. While a number of interesting approaches are being taken to evaluation of risky investment programs, I believe we have a good way yet to go.

I do not mean to imply that the conceptual problems of dealing with uncertainty and risk make quantitative analysis valueless; quite the contrary. Analysis can help bare the consequences of alternative plans. I believe, however, that development of concepts for analyzing uncertain returns from investment programs is a most intriguing and challenging research field.

CONCLUSION

Interest in physical distribution systems is growing widely. I have suggested that quantitative studies can help clarify conflicts in policies and functional objectives, and have indicated some of the concepts I believe are fruitful in a systematic study of physical distribution. I have tried to show how these concepts can be brought to bear on many issues in a distribution system, and to demonstrate that quantitative studies of physical distribution must rest on detailed observations of the particular system and market. Development of study concepts and techniques is a vital topic; though much progress has been made to develop methods having practical value now, we have opportunity for a good deal of work particularly in development of long-range programming techniques.

9. LOGISTICS OF PHYSICAL FACILITIES IN DISTRIBUTION*

Alfred A. Kuehn

CHARACTERISTICS OF DISTRIBUTION AND TRANSPORTATION PROBLEMS

Distribution and transportation problems tend to require the examination of large quantities of data. Simple rules are seldom available to compute the large bulk of information needed in solving such problems. For example, transportation rates from point to point are generally the result of a long process of negotiation, competition and historical circumstance rather than a convenient function of air-mile or even road-mile distances. Special commodity rates are generally negotiated prior to the construction of a new plant or warehouse. Price breaks at various volumes are frequently open to bargaining between large-volume shippers and transport firms.

Even greater volumes of other types of data are likely to be required in the solution of many distribution problems: expected demand of individual or groups of customers, warehouse operating costs, effect of delivery delays upon lost sales, etc. For example, in the scheduling of airlines it is necessary to know the daily and hourly distribution of traffic demand between city A and city B as well as the attractive potential of competitors' planes and flight schedules. All of these factors result in a very complex problem both in terms of data requirements and in terms of a model capable of capturing the essence of the problem.

ALTERNATIVE APPROACHES TO THE SOLUTION OF DISTRIBUTION PROBLEMS

Two general classes of quantitative methods have been used to solve distribution and transportation problems: (1) optimizing algorithms such as linear and integer programming, and (2) heuristic programs.

*From *Marketing and Economic Development,* American Marketing Association, September, 1965, pp. 688–95.

The use of heuristics in the solution of such problems is the older of the two methods, businessmen having used such an approach for years. The main shortcoming of the average businessman's use of heuristics is his dependence upon his personal computational abilities rather than those of a high-speed electronic computer. (Another shortcoming of the businessman is his failure to coin and/or use the term "heuristics." The term heuristics has made respectable a method still known by most businessmen as "cut and try" or "trial and error.") To be sure, recent developments in heuristic programming have improved greatly upon the rules of thumb used by many businessmen, but this would appear to be only of secondary significance. If businessmen once attain command over the computer, they too are likely to develop improved guides for decision making.

Optimizing models, developed and put into business practice largely since World War II, have been the province of operations researchers. Recently, however, heuristic methods have also been adopted and promoted by this group of "management scientists" as providing a means of solving business problems which have resisted solution by the available optimizing methods. All too frequently, business problems cannot be cast into the framework required by optimizing models.

CONDITIONS AFFECTING CHOICE BETWEEN HEURISTIC
AND OPTIMIZING MODELS

The most desirable attribute of optimizing models is the guarantee that the computational method they prescribe leads to the best possible solution (or set of solutions) of the problem *as it has been stated in the model.* Knowledge that the optimal solution has or has not been obtained can be a valuable bit of information.

Heuristic methods do not as a rule guarantee reaching the optimal solution (or set of solutions) and, furthermore, do not provide an indication as to whether or not the optimal solution has been obtained. The value of heuristic methods lies elsewhere:

1. *Complexity*—heuristic methods can be used to solve much more complex problems than can be treated by existing optimizing models.
2. *Size*—heuristic methods can be used to solve problems which are much larger than those which can currently be solved on existing computing equipment with the available optimizing models.
3. *Cost*—heuristic methods can solve problems economically which could only be solved at prohibitive cost by available optimizing models.

Heuristic methods are tools that can be very valuable in solving today's business problems. The standards of comparison in such cases are current practice and other available alternatives—not the unattainable guarantee of an optimal solution. Heuristic methods can be used in solving all business problems which can be explicitly and unambiguously stated and for which procedures can be specified to search for (generate) and evaluate alternatives. Heuristic programs can be developed to solve such problems faster, with greater accuracy, and with better results than human problem solvers insofar as we are capable of identifying (or improving upon) methods in current use.

For the future, there is reason to believe that heuristic and optimizing models will be integrated into individual programs. Heuristic methods might be used to develop advanced starting points for subsequent analysis by optimizing models, or the latter might be used merely to test whether an optimal solution has been reached. Even greater integration is likely insofar as optimizing algorithms are incorporated as subroutines within heuristic programs. This approach, for example, would appear to be one of the alternative ways in which certain types of capacity constraints could be introduced into the plant and warehouse location problem discussed briefly in the next section.

Warehouse and plant location problem

Several versions of this heuristic program have been in use for more than four years. Consequently, it has been documented in more detail than the other two problems and programs which are outlined in the following sections. Much of the program structure as it exists today is comparable to that originally published in "A Heuristic Program for Locating Warehouses."[1] Some of the more recent revisions and additional details in its application have been documented by P. L. Flannery in "Heuristic Warehouse and Plant Location Programs: Applications Guide."[2] Consequently, the discussion in this section will be limited to certain general observations about the performance of the program in practical application, the experience of some of the firms who have used it, and the problems and costs of data processing and the preparation of input data.

The performance of the program has exceeded our wildest expectations in terms of the quality of solutions provided. Although a large amount of research has been done in additional testing of the general form of the heuristics used in the original program, only very limited success has been achieved in terms of improving the quality of solutions. Much more progress has been made in reprogramming the problem for greater computational efficiency, application to much larger problems, and development of improved input and output formats to facilitate practical application. Also, in reprogramming, the program was prepared so that it could be adapted quite easily to a much wider range of problems than had been originally anticipated. Every application

---

[1]A. A. Kuehn and M. J. Hamburger, "A Heuristic Program for Locating Warehouses," *Management Science*, Vol. IX, No. 4, July, 1963.

[2]P. L. Flannery, *Heuristic Warehouse and Plant Location Programs: Applications Guide* (Pittsburgh, Pa.: Market Science Associates, Inc., 1964).

appears to require some program modifications and, consequently, a variety of new cost functions, constraints, and the like have been developed for use with the various individual versions of the program. It was discovered that the program was not only useful in analyzing warehousing networks but also multiple locations of plants (e.g., refineries, assembly plants, etc.), alternative types of warehousing or plant facilities, and different modes of shipping. Mixing points at plants can also be evaluated.

The experience of firms using the program has been very favorable in that great opportunities have been uncovered for improvement of distribution systems. In large complex networks, management is likely to have considered only localized changes in operational procedures and so is unlikely to uncover the desirability of major changes in its distribution system. Another result of the program has been to focus management's attention on existing transportation rate structures which are out of line. In several cases, solutions provided by the program appeared to be completely unreasonable, but further inspection identified the problem as peculiarities in rate structure. In some cases, identification of such factors can provide direction to management in the renegotiation of rates. The program can then also be valuable in the evaluation of the total impact on costs of any proposed rate changes.

One firm has also made much use of the program in the evaluation of the various stages of their distribution network as it might change from the current existing system toward the best system originally developed by the heuristic approach. Organizational and transition problems required a step-by-step adjustment. Also, since only half of the proposed changes are likely to result in 85 to 90 percent of the total potential cost savings, even neglecting transition costs, it is likely that all of the proposed changes will never be instituted. The errors in input data, coupled with transition costs and the fact that the actual problem is changing over time, tend to suggest that management should not arbitrarily attempt to institute the "best" solution developed by the program but rather only move in that direction, reevaluating its position along the way.

The major problem in the use of the program is the collection of data. Problems as large as ten factories, 46 intermediate transfer points and 287 district warehouses have been run through the computer at a computational cost of only $400 to $500. The evaluation of specific networks is substantially less expensive. Consequently, the major problem apart from defining the problem is collecting the needed data and preparing it for use with the computer. Although this can be an enormous task, the response of the firms that have gone to the effort of doing so indicates that the result that can be achieved from a reevaluation of warehouse locations and operating patterns represents a very good return on the investment. Some firms now look upon the reevaluation of warehousing and distribution systems as an item to be reviewed annually rather than only when costs are already out of line.

LOCAL TRUCK ROUTING AND SCHEDULING

The routing and scheduling of trucks is a problem which must be solved very rapidly once orders have been received. For a local distributor with 35 10-ton and 20-ton trucks and a total of 400 customers, it has been established that even a crude heuristic program can meet all delivery requirements and substantially reduce the overtime costs of the drivers and helpers.

The problem in this case is to group the orders and route the trucks to minimize costs, given the available truck capacities, union rules for drivers and helpers, travel time between customers, unloading times, and state regulations on axle weights. Orders must be processed rapidly and instructions provided to the warehouse order fillers, dock loaders, and drivers and helpers. The time period currently available for these decisions is so short that management has relied upon the use of relatively stable route structures as a means of meeting the customers' delivery requirements. Nevertheless, changes in the daily order sizes on these routes offer the opportunity for the development of a more flexible scheduling procedure to make better use of the available facilities and manpower resources. It appears that a substantial increase in the delivery capacity of the firm could be achieved in this manner, providing savings in the investment in trucks as well as in daily operating costs.

A computer program now operating but still under development in conjunction with R. L. Hayes, Carnegie Institute of Technology, approaches the truck-routing problem by identifying extreme points to which deliveries must be made and then filling out the truck capacity and guaranteed union working hours in a near-optimal way. Orders to be added to the delivery route on any given day are chosen probabilistically, the probability of any given order being selected for addition depending upon its suitability as a filler order, the ease with which it might be added to the routes, and the incremental cost of adding it to the route in question. The total scheduling program is reprocessed a number of times, in effect resolving the problem on each cycle, until there is reasonable assurance that a good solution has been developed.

AIRLINE SCHEDULING

A number of optimizing models for use in solving this problem have been reported in the literature in recent years. Interestingly enough, however, the airlines are not using the techniques that have been published. Several of the major airlines have pointed to the major problem —the techniques do not recognize the time distribution of demand between specific cities. The "solutions" merely schedule planes to provide the number of daily flights requested by management but do not schedule these flights with a view toward the time distribution of demand or competitive schedules.

Most of the proposed solutions are recognized by their developers as not solving the complete problem. It has been suggested, for example, that the solutions provided are only suggested solutions which must be "hand-massaged" to develop practical operating schedules. This does not really appear to be desirable in practice, however, since only a very limited number of minor local changes could be made without disrupting the entire schedule. When one flight is changed, it is likely to conflict with the future deployment of that plane.

A heuristic program now in development for the airline scheduling problem recognizes explicitly (1) the size and time distribution of passenger demand between each pair of cities on the airline's CAB flight authorization, (2) CAB restrictions on route structures and flight requirements, (3) plane maintenance requirements, and (4) competitive schedules, including types of planes. Not yet included are two important issues which will be considered at a future date, the scheduling of flight crews and the effects of pattern scheduling upon consumer choice (e.g., a flight between New York and Chicago every hour on the hour). Within the framework of the above variables, the program is designed to schedule an airline's planes to "near optimize" management's criterion function (e.g., profits, share of market on individual routes subject to some minimum profit constraint, etc.). Thus the program determines how many flights to schedule and when to schedule them in an attempt to best satisfy management's objectives. If management wishes to add additional flights (or reduce the number of flights) on particular route segments, this can be incorporated into the problem as a constraint much as can changes in CAB directives.

The program begins operation by scheduling a plane from some major terminal on the airline's route structure to some other city consistent with CAB restrictions. In choosing which city to fly to, the program considers all the available alternatives over the next two stages. That is, consideration is given not only to the profitability of the alternative flights that might now be scheduled out of City A but also the profitability available in scheduling the plane over the subsequent leg of its journey out of the destination city. An additional alternative is offered if no flights are profitable and if the plane is not needed in another city, namely, delaying the flight until a more profitable level of demand is available.

The daily distribution of demand is identified as 48 values, representing half-hourly intervals beginning at 12:15 A.M. each day. It appears that the time distribution of demand over all city pairs can be classified into no more than 25 sets of values. The passengers attracted by a given airline's flight from City A to City B at time t with a stop at City C will then depend upon the total demand and its distribution, the availability of competitive flights at various departure times, the time delay en route of each competitor, the type of planes, and the airline's connecting route structure at cities A and B. The available traffic is divided among competitors according to a mathematical relationship previously found useful in describing consumer preferences and choice behavior in the purchase of grocery products differing with respect to certain physical characteristics. In the airline problem, the times of departure, times en route and types of planes would appear to be the most significant variables. (Note that the types of planes and times en route can incorporate much of what would otherwise appear to be a significant effect —the number of stops. Additional empirical evidence is necessary to establish whether the number of stops must be considered as an additional variable to take into account effects above and beyond that of the plane type and route times.)

While this is still a matter of conjecture, there is reason to believe that the program now under development will prove useful in the development of airline schedules. Much more work is, however, required to incorporate maintenance and crew scheduling, matters of serious concern to the airlines. These too, however, should be solvable.

Other uses of the program could include evaluation of the probable effects of CAB route changes, the determination of fleet sizes, and questions related to the mix of planes. Extension of the program should also permit improved solutions to the deployment of planes when schedules must be violated due to weather, mechanical failure, and the like.

CONCLUSION

This brief review of research in the location and scheduling of physical distribution facilities has pointed to the promise shown by heuristic methods. The location of warehouses was discussed as an example of an application already implemented with favorable results by a number of major firms. Truck and airline scheduling were presented as large, complex problems which will soon be solved by heuristic computer programs, operating programs now being available for test purposes. Each of these applications has been demonstrated to have the potential of producing significant reductions in distribution and transportation expenses.

The prime hurdles restricting the development and use of heuristic programs are (1) sound statements or models of transportation and distribution problems are not generally available, (2) the quality of heuristic solutions is difficult to establish, being dependent upon comparison with other known solutions, with no guarantee of an "optimum" or even good solution, and (3) procedures by which useful heuristics might be developed or identified are not well established. At this stage of the development of heuristic programming, research with heuristic methods is more of an art than a science. Nevertheless, the great potential of heuristic programs in helping to solve the complex problems of distribution and transportation management is likely to insure the widespread use of such techniques within the next few years.

10. FORCES INFLUENCING FINISHED INVENTORY DISTRIBUTION*

Donald J. Bowersox

INTRODUCTION

Executives are experts—experts in the art of administering corporate resources and in achieving corporate profits. For this basic reason it is not surprising that increasing managerial talent is being directed toward the perplexities of spiraling distribution costs. Within this neglected maze of interdepartmental administration, executives have uncovered a new and rewarding arena for applying techniques of scientific management.

PHYSICAL DISTRIBUTION DEFINED

Physical distribution, broadly defined, is that dimension of management responsible for designing and administering systems devoted to controlling the movement of raw materials and finished inventories in a manner consistent with long-run corporate objectives. Distribution management trespasses and embodies elements of most corporate decision-making centers. It is a team function concerned with the timing of material and finished inventory transfer. The objective of distribution management is to place the right quantity of the right assets at the right place in a manner timely to meet sales and production requirements at the lowest possible total cost.

PHYSICAL DISTRIBUTION IS A TEAM FUNCTION

It is important to realize that efficient distribution management is a team function demanding holistic corporate effort. Entirely too much managerial talent and time has dribbled down the bottomless cup of organizational semantics. From these fruitless attempts to identify and structure a single position in the corporate pyramid as the sole managerial control of physical distribution one single and readily apparent fact has emerged. No one man or one department can possibly possess

*From *The Social Responsibilities of Marketing,* American Marketing Association, December, 1961, pp. 491–97.

sufficient technical knowledge, insight or information to direct all logistical activities related to market planning, purchasing, transportation, warehouse operations, inventory management, production planning, packaging, material handling and other aspects of corporate distribution management. Each is a technical and complicated field of professional endeavor requiring the full-time attention of competent specialists.

What is needed in business today is not another "Parkinsonian Empire." Rather, the complex demands of modern business management require:

(1) An overall corporate sensitivity to the needs for highest interdepartmental coordination between the many specialized areas of management influential in successful distribution management.

(2) A functional method of distribution cost accounting capable of adjusting interdepartmental cost tradeoffs on a corporate-wide basis.

Only when total corporate management becomes distribution-oriented and when accounting records are capable of accurately evaluating would-be "heroes" and "reluctant villains" on a systemwide basis will management truly stand ready to strangle nonproductive distribution expense.

MARKETING AND ITS NEGLECTED RESPONSIBILITY

This brief excursion into organization may appear far afield from marketing and other forces which influence distribution system design. However, it is not. Among the many managers who have neglected their physical distribution responsibility, the marketing manager is outstanding. Regardless of the fundamental need for coordination between demand creation and physical fulfillments in the marketplace, marketing executives and educators have historically neglected physical distribution. Only the most recent of marketing texts discuss physical distribution as a marketing function. Few institutions of higher learning have followed Michigan State University's leadership in offering physical distribution courses as part of the marketing curriculum.

Distribution management has two basic sides—raw material management and finished inventory management. Programs designed to control finished inventory management center around one series of related decisions—when, where, and in what quantity to physically locate products. The only sound answer to this vexing problem must emanate from market intelligence. The marketing manager must outline a broad program of finished inventory distribution since he and only he has the prime responsibility of coordinating corporate marketing programs.

It is the responsibility of the marketing department to issue inventory directives based upon knowledge of planned marketing efforts. The detail of satisfying market inventory requirements is properly the responsibility of specialists concerned with each functional aspect of physical distribution. The traffic manager, for example, is not in a position to predict inventory demands. But, given a clear communique of marketing requirements, the traffic manager is an expert in the technique of transporting inventory. It is the responsibility of marketing managers to coordinate all such types of technical know-how into an integrated marketing effort.

THE NEED FOR A MARKETING ORIENTATION

Distribution policies established by firms pursuing scientific inventory management clearly illustrate the requirement for customized programs to satisfy individual marketing demands.

Trends reflecting the number of distribution centers required to meet market demands vary by industries as well as between firms in similar industries. The choice between holding field or centralized inventories depends upon particular forces influencing each individual firm. Countless cases can be illustrated of firms increasing the number of distribution centers while others—even competitors—are pursuing a program of warehouse reduction. Many such adjustments initially began from a near equal number of warehouses for all major firms within particular industries.

The question of what to hold in field inventory depots also reflects contradictory trends. For example, one firm supplies consumer replacement parts. Their distribution policy is to adhere strictly to a program of echeloning inventories at various distances from the marketplace. The slower the part turnover the more centralized the inventory. The slowest moving parts are held at one central location which services the entire world.

In contrast a second firm, which supplies industrial replacement parts, follows a completely opposite distribution policy. In order to meet unexpected demands this second firm holds sufficient quantities of all slow movers at each field inventory location. In contrast to the first firm, fast- and medium-turnover products are supplied on a regular basis direct to customers from plants and central supply centers.

This differential in policy is easily explained when one examines the market each firm serves and the degree of product differentiation each enjoys. The first firm faces extensive competition on replacement parts on new models. However, as the original product ages this competition decreases, making his firm the only supplier. The second firm, on the other hand, sells a product with very little style deterioration and which has a high degree of competitive substitutability. In this firm's market, a supplier is measured by purchasing agents with respect to how fast unexpected production breakdowns can be remedied.

Each firm faces a different marketing problem and each follows a different distribution policy with respect to finished product inventories. Many other cases could be cited to illustrate the need for customized distribution programs. While many trends may appear on the surface to be contradictory, they are not. Each program evolved from detailed analysis of what the marketing needs of the particular firm are and how they could be most economically satisfied. The final program developed to render integrated marketing a reality depends upon the combined impact of environmental, managerial, and competitive forces.

ENVIRONMENTAL FORCES

Environmental or ecological forces influencing distribution policy are external to the firm. While the firm may exercise some control over the impact of these forces over time, they are generally considered constant during a given planning period. Environmental forces are summarized as follows:

(1) *Industry Competitive Structure*—Most industrial and/or consumer marketing is conducted under monopolistic or oligopolistic conditions of imperfect competition. When competition is to a degree imperfect, distribution offers a method of differentiating a firm's market offer. To the degree that an industry tends toward the extremes of pure competition or monopoly the importance of finished inventory distribution as a competitive weapon diminishes.

(2) *Market Differentials*—Markets vary in terms of quantity of purchasing power. Each firm attempts to isolate various segments of the total market as the "core" of their overall product market. Core market targets in relation to overall marketing effort represent one basic determinant of when and where to hold customized inventory mixtures. As the relative importance of a market diminishes, the tendency is toward centralized inventories with the reverse being true as volume increases.

(3) *Network of Service Industries*—Goods must flow to market through common contract of private carrier networks. In many cases products flow through public warehouses. The array of available service industries and their alternative capabilities constitutes a restraint upon the freedom enjoyed in planning finished inventory policies.

(4) *Legal Structure*—Legal parameters prevail at each stage of physical distribution. Such forces determine the freedom a firm enjoys in planning distribution policy. Most prevalent in physical distribution is the body of law regulating inter-city product movement.

(5) *Economic Forces*—The general level of economic activity has a profound impact upon when and where inventory is placed. On a regional basis economic fluctuation greatly influences inventory mix by acting as an independent governor on particular product turnover.

MANAGERIAL FORCES

Managerial forces influencing distribution policy are reflected by corporate goals as well as immediate past-distribution decisions. Such managerial forces are considered short-run, being fixed for varying lengths of the planning period.

(1) *Marketing Programs*—Managerial decisions concerning pricing, promotional mix, product mix, and channel strategy represent restraints within which finished inventory management must be programmed and controlled. Decisions concerning each aspect of the total marketing effort should be formulated, in part, upon physical distribution considerations. However, once an integrated marketing program is developed, finished inventory must be managed in a manner which complements all aspects of the total marketing effort.

(2) *Locational Structure*—Efficient and strategic inventory management must be conducted within a network of given locational points. These locations may be private or public and may be integrated through channel negotiations. The degree of fixity varies, with production location being most fixed, and retail locations being most variable. Normally, locations remain fixed during a given marketing period.

(3) *Immediate Past-distribution Decisions*—All inventory dispersements are made under conditions of uncertainty. Consequently they represent "risky" decisions subject to a high degree of misallocation. At any given time in a distribution program immediate decisions must be based, in part, upon immediate past history—good or bad. Inventory transfer costs are "ratchet-like" in nature meaning that the optimal result in final analysis is a rare occurrence. The typical distribution program represents a suboptimization of current demands in relation to past errors. The higher the degree of inventory centralization, the lower the occurrence of suboptimization.

COMPETITIVE FORCES

Competitive tactics, regardless of soundness, cast an important influence upon a firm's inventory decisions. An uneconomical inventory move on the part of a major competitor may force instantaneous reaction. Depending upon a great variety of factors, a firm may be forced to duplicate competitive moves simply to prevent consumer switchover. The degree to which this is true depends primarily upon the service elasticity of demand for the product mix in question. This need to duplicate competitive moves is offset by the extent to which the firm's products enjoy real or imaginary differentials in the eyes of the customer.

CONCLUSION

In conclusion, forces which influence finished inventory distribution systems may be categorized as environmental, managerial and competitive. The impact of these forces creates a maze of interwoven factors from which each firm must develop a customized distribution program.

Because of his basic awareness of market requirements, the marketing executive stands in a pivotal position to coordinate a firm's inventory exposure to markets and competition. Historically, marketing men have neglected this responsibility. To be assured of an integrated marketing effort, the marketing manager must direct the "what," "when" and "where" of finished goods distribution. The details of "how" remain the rightful concern of other specialists. In final analysis, physical distribution is a team function demanding holistic management attention.

11. A CLOSER LOOK AT OPERATIONS RESEARCH*

Philip A. Doherty

This article deals with three major features of operations research: the concept of the problem, the approach, and some techniques.

CONCEPTS OF OPERATIONS RESEARCH

Two prinicpal factors have been responsible for the development of the O.R. (operations research) concept of the business problem: *growth* and *pace*.

As growth and diversification have progressed and the pace of doing business has accelerated, the manager's problems have become more complex, and he has less time in which to make decisions. The number of factors to be considered is constantly increasing; and the data now available, however voluminous, inadequately inform him on these factors.

THE NEW CONCEPT: INTEGRATION

Consider one action: the sale of a single item. This transaction will be processed through or affect every segment of the business. The item ordered will be removed from inventory and shipped. The accumulation of inventory depletions will initiate a replenishment order, which in turn will produce a manufacturing schedule and call for more raw materials. A succession of such manufacturing orders will require maintenance and ultimate replacement or expansion of facilities.

Product quality must be maintained and products developed which will enable the firm to maintain or to improve its competitive position.

Each item shipped must be billed, and records of customer accounts receivable maintained. Inventories and facilities for shipment of orders must be financed. These requirements are related to sales forecasts, which in part are based on histories of accumulations of customer or-

---

°*Journal of Marketing*, April, 1963, pp. 59–65.

ders, and in part on marketing research. Finally, the successful order immediately "signals" the marketing activity to take steps to generate more orders.

These expressed relationships demand an organizational concept which, in spite of lip service, has not yet been really accepted. That concept is *integration*.

INTEGRATION VS. COMPARTMENTALIZATION

The traditional concept of company organization is expressed in the form of the usual organization chart, which may itself have helped to perpetuate operation on a compartmentalized basis, with each manager concentrating primarily on his own segment of the problem.

Organizations often claim to have established horizontal lines of communication by committee or by management directive; but considerations of proprietorship, self-protection, empire building, and inade-

FIGURE 1

SCHEMATIC DIAGRAM, INVENTORY MANAGEMENT SYSTEM

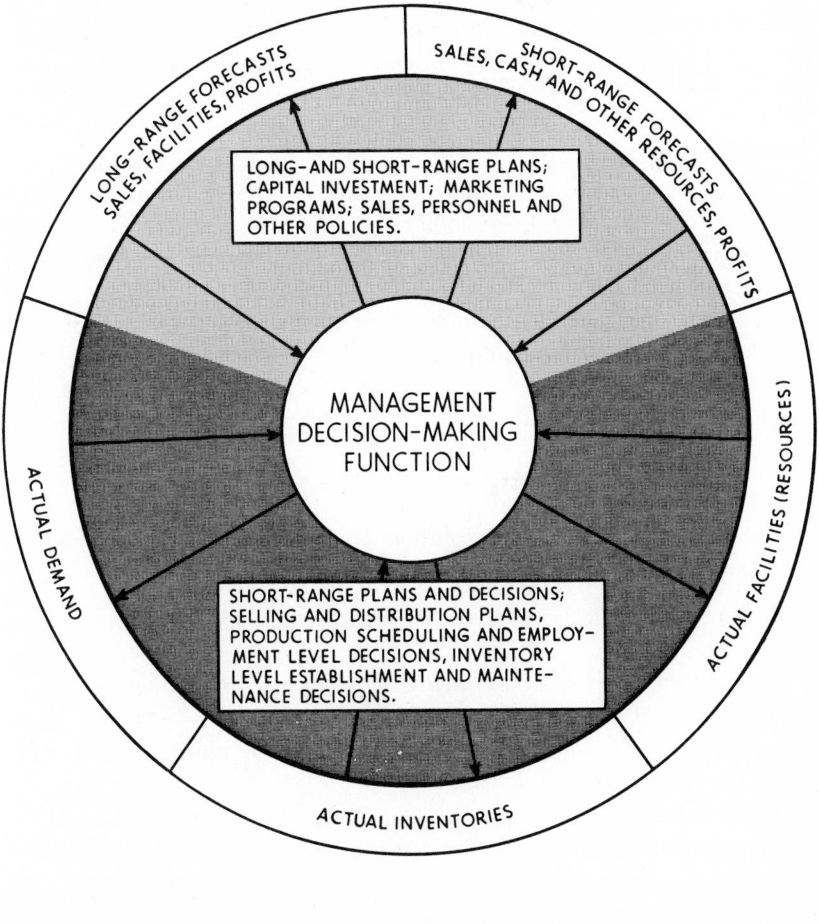

quate attempts to perform a single function without integration may reduce such "lines of communication" to ineffectiveness.

By contrast, the O.R. concept views the corporation as an organic whole, existing in an economic and sociological environment. It considers the problems of the corporation in the perspective of this environment and implications posed by this environment in the solution of these problems. Within the corporation, operations research similarly studies the interactions of the various functions, quantifies them, and determines their effects on the solutions proposed.

Visually, we might represent the O.R. concept of the organization as a wheel—with management the policy-making hub, obtaining data from and providing direction to its established supporting functions through the spokes.

A CONCRETE ILLUSTRATION

We may express this concept of functional interactions more tangibly by the problem of planning product inventories, illustrated in Figure 1.[1]

The exhibit shows only some of the factors involved. Obviously neither long-range nor short-range inventory planning decisions can be made until the corresponding sales forecasts have been provided, and until the actual demand, having a known reliability, has been estimated. Supporting these must be the functions of marketing research and line sales effort.

Once forecasts of demand and marketing plans are determined, policy and operating decisions may be made which encompass not only inventory planning but every other facet of the business as well—the use, acquisition, or disposition of manpower, money, machinery, materials, and methods.

Operations research is thus more than an assortment of sophisticated, complex mathematical techniques for solving isolated, unrelated problems. Until its conceptual aspect is understood and applied, use of the available techniques will fall short of the full potential of this approach.

THE O.R. APPROACH

The O.R. approach to the solution of the business problem may be described as a series of sequential steps:

Identification and description of the problem and the objectives of the solution.
Representation of the problem in the form of a mathematical model.
Quantification of the problem variables.
Reduction of the variables to a workable total, by elimination of those of little significance or sensitivity.

---

[1]Based on the inventory planning model contained in John F. Magee, *Production Planning and Control* (New York: McGraw-Hill Book Co., Inc., 1958), chap. 1.

Manipulation of the model under varying conditions, assumptions, and
policy restrictions.
Analysis and presentation of the sets of results obtained.
Evaluation of decisions based on these results.

Many persons consider the two italicized steps—involving the quantification of a problem within a model—the essence of O.R.

It should be emphasized that the operations researcher is not the decision maker. He supplies management with analyses of the quantitative
factors implicit in the problem; and he provides alternative solutions,
including evaluations of their costs and impacts. He thus makes it possible for management to assume its true role—the consideration of families of decisions, by which many individual routine decisions may be
delegated, even mechanized.

OPERATIONS RESEARCH DEFINED

Operations research has been defined in many different ways, but
one of the best definitions is: "Systematic inquiry into operating problems for the purpose of predicting quantitatively the operating conditions under which optimum results may be achieved, thereby developing
sound quantitative bases for management decisions."[2]

Since business problems may not on the surface appear to be sus-
ceptible to formal analysis, management may find it difficult to select
and measure the problem criteria and to assign relative values to in-
tangible problem variables. It is also difficult to determine the probability of risk or degrees of uncertainty which must be included in the
model, since precise information on these matters seldom exists.

What makes the O.R. approach possible is the basic similarity of
most business problems—"the determination of the best (optimum) distribution of a group of limited resources, among a group of competing
requirements, within a common set of fixed limits."[3]

THE MATHEMATICAL MODEL

O.R. frequently represents the business problem in terms of the
"mathematical model." This has been defined by many writers simply
as that system of equations which describes a business problem.

Although new to the solution of business problems, the use of models
is certainly not new to industry. In the study of aircraft design, for example, extensive use is made of wind-tunnel models. In ship design,
hull models are tested in tanks—mathematically formulated curves are
constructed at each frame, from bow to stern, and lines of the hull are

[2]Developed by H. W. Martin, associate professor of management engineering,
Rensselaer Polytechnic Institute, Troy, N. Y.

[3]Alexander Henderson and Robert Schleifer, "Mathematical Programming: Better
Information for Better Decision Making," *Harvard Business Review*, Vol. 32 (May-
June, 1954).

faired into these curves between frames. The model thus approximates, between stations, the formulated curves of these stations, and it is assumed that no more significantly accurate results could be obtained by solving for curves between stations.

Similarly, the business model need not duplicate every configuration of the real world which it represents, although it must *approximate* those conditions realistically. The problem solutions will then approximate the optimum closely enough to be valid.

Further, we do not always need actual data in the solution of a model. In many problems, simulated data (even random data) may provide the solutions sought.

While not all problems can be represented in model form, there are proved rules for those which can be so described. These rules permit us to know *positively* the degree of probability that we will reach the best solution, and it will be absolutely clear how this solution has been reached. Alternatively, by these rules we can identify the problems for which there is *no solution* or *no best solution*.

Specifically, our business model may take the form of a chart, graph, array, table of values, or a system of one or more equations. Each of these forms is derived from equations, or may be reduced to equations. An equation is the basic vehicle, manipulated by every O.R. technique, to resolve the problem described.

TWO SAMPLE MODELS

Our first example is a production planning model—basically a marketing problem based on a sales forecast.

An extreme simplification of a production planning system allows us to express a model in equation form:

$$P_Q = S_Q + (P_{Q-1} - S_Q) + (I_Q - I_{Q-1})$$

In this model, planned production is expressed as functions of forecast sales, previous excess or inadequate production, and anticipated inventory adjustments, since:

$P_Q =$ production planned for the coming quarter.

$S_Q =$ Sales forecast for the coming quarter.

$P_{Q-1} - S_Q =$ Last quarter's production related to coming quarter forecast sales.

$I_Q - I_{Q-1} =$ Coming quarter inventory compared with last quarter actual inventory.

In the model, all functional relationships are linear, although were it to be more fully developed these relationships might well become of second or higher order. The objective of optimization, although implied, is not conclusively proved.

Our second example is a better illustration of the process of optimization. This is an economic order quantity (EOQ) model, in the solution of which calculus may be used.

Differential calculus is an easy way to determine an optimum solution, since it allows us to reduce a function (the interrelation of two variables) to its first derivative, which by definition is the slope of the function at any point. Equating this function to zero (zero slope describes the horizontal) and solving, we find the value of the function at the point of horizontal slope, a maximum or minimum value, which represents the "optimum" solution.

This is shown by the economic order quantity model (Figure 2), representing a quadratic function (equation 1), the first derivative of which (equation 2) describes the most economic (minimum total cost per unit) lot to make or buy within the parameters of sales demand, setup cost, inventory cost, and acquisition cost.[4]

FIGURE 2

ECONOMIC LOT SIZE MODEL

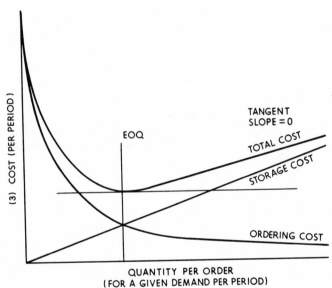

Not discussed fully here but of some interest is the rate-of-change model, frequently used to evaluate the effectiveness of advertising programs and salesmen's efforts. It is a quantitative model of customer activity and provides a method for describing mathematically the anticipated switching of customers and noncustomers in a potential market.

[4]Richard B. Maffei, "Mathematical Models, Values of Parameters, and the Sensitivity Analysis of Management Decision Rules," *Journal of Marketing*, Vol. 21 (April, 1957), pp. 419–27.

It further provides a means of evaluating the effects of imposed factors, such as advertising, on sales programs.[5]

SOME O.R. TECHNIQUES

The rapid development of O.R. and its extensions to the business world has entailed the formalization of many techniques. These have been successfully applied to finite engineering problems (such as turbine design) and to product problems and process research problems, as well as to business problems. Some of the more important techniques are:

1. Mathematical statistics—including time series analysis and regression analysis.
2. Mathematical programming—including linear, nonlinear, and dynamic programming.
3. Simulation—including operational gaming or business games, and Monte Carlo analysis.
4. Network theory including program evaluation and review techniques (PERT), critical path method (CPM), and line of balance (LOB).
5. Queuing theory.
6. Game theory.
7. Electronic data processing (EDP).

MATHEMATICAL STATISTICS

The designs of experiments and investigations have long been based on mathematical statistics. In addition, the laws of probability, combination, distribution, and expected values have been used for years in quality control, market analysis and other business functions. The industrial engineer, for example, has developed statistical inferences based on assumed distribution probabilities, to prepare sampling plans for the continuing evaluation of product quality, thus substantially reducing product inspection required to ensure maintenance of desired outgoing quality levels. Later in this article, a description of a sales forecasting model discusses regression analysis, another form of mathematical statistics.[6]

MATHEMATICAL PROGRAMMING

Mathematical programming is that method of optimizing, for a given objective (function), within established limits (parameters), any interacting set of conditions (interacting problem variables). It can require the use of matrix algebra and differential calculus. Programming can be:

[5]John F. Magee, "Operations Research in Making Marketing Decisions," *Journal of Marketing*, Vol. 25 (October, 1960), pp. 18–23.

[6]Alexander McFarlane Wood, *Introduction to the Theory of Statistics* (McGraw-Hill Book Co., Inc., 1950).

Linear, in which all relationships can be expressed in directly proportional terms (for example, relationship of input to output would be
a straight line if graphed).

Nonlinear, encompassing nonlinear (for example, $y = x^2$) problem variables and expressed graphically as a curve.

Dynamic, developing conditional optimum solutions for each phase of
a problem, progressing in single steps, using the output from each
step as the input to the next to arrive at a final optimum solution.

SIMULATION

Simulation is a trial-and-error technique of manipulating mathematical
models to determine the effect of decisions in response to the conditions
described by the model, over a given period of time.

Operational gaming, more frequently described as business gaming,
is a simulation experiment in which the outcomes of strategies in interacting competitive situations, based on intuitive decisions, are developed.
They are tested by including personnel as decision makers during the
running of the experiment.[7]

In *Monte Carlo analysis,* data are generated by use of a random number generator, according to some known pattern of randomness from
the real world. It is the basis of formulating the inputs to many simulation experiments.

NETWORK THEORY

PERT is one of a number of forms of network theory. With CPM,
LOB, and other techniques, it provides a means of maximizing the
effectiveness of project scheduling, evaluating the relationships of project
functions, determining which are critical to project completion—hence,
the development of the "critical path." It also provides a means of determining the effects on resources, such as manpower or money, of revising project schedules, and of alternative allocation of resources.
Finally, it provides a means of evaluating project progress.[8]

QUEUING THEORY

Queuing theory, applicable to waiting lines, is the technique of establishing service priorities for units arriving at a given point, balancing
the costs of waiting against the costs of providing the service required.

GAME THEORY

Game theory is the technique of determining the best strategy for
one of two or more opponents in competitive situations where the out-

[7] Oliver B. Schenk, "Mathematical Models of Market Simulation," *Journal of Marketing,* Vol. 24 (April, 1960), pp. 69–74.

[8] George A. W. Boehm, "Helping the Executive to Make up His Mind," *Fortune,* Vol. 55 (April, 1962), pp. 128–31, 218, 222, and 224.

comes of various strategies can be precisely predicted. It has assisted management successfully to determine the timing of advertising programs and the allocation of funds of competing types of advertising media.[9]

ELECTRONIC DATA PROCESSING

EDP is established as a separate category because it makes many O.R. solutions possible. This is not to say that O.R. cannot be used unless we have a computer; some problems do not require one, and service bureaus can handle others. However, it would be difficult to solve many of the integrated, complex business problems so appropriate to operations research without the ability of the computer to handle and process large amounts of data quickly.

CLASSIC O.R. MODELS

Some of these techniques have been used so frequently that "classical" models have been developed. Although named for their most common applications, these models are useful in many functions not specifically identified. For most, computer programs are available through equipment manufacturers and service bureaus. Some of these "classical" models are next described.

Sales forecasting model.   Figure 3 illustrates a statistical sales forecasting model. If we have a time series analysis of the sales of a given product and the corresponding movement of an "influencing" index, we can determine the existence and degree of correlation between the two by means of regression analysis. Thence, we can develop a product sales forecast based on the forecast of the index.

A condition of uncertainty might call for Monte Carlo analysis in the manipulation of this model. If we did not have a product sales history by the required increments but did know the average historical sales and their probable distribution, we could generate data by use of some random number generator. This would provide a hypothetical sales pattern having the same statistical character as the actual experience, at less cost and less time than developing the actual data would require.[10]

Replacement model.   The replacement model is used to determine replacement schedules for equipment to minimize costs of new equipment, maintenance of existing equipment, and equipment down time. Preventive maintenance scheduling is a special case of the replacement model.

---

[9]Cyril B. Herrman and John B. Stewart, "The Experimental Game," *Journal of Marketing*, Vol. 22 (July, 1957), pp. 12–20.

[10]The application of Monte Carlo analysis to the sales forecasting model is described further in Werner F. Hirsch, "Decision Making in Industrial Marketing," *Journal of Marketing*, Vol. 24 (January, 1960), pp. 21–27.

FIGURE 3

SALES FORECASTING MODEL

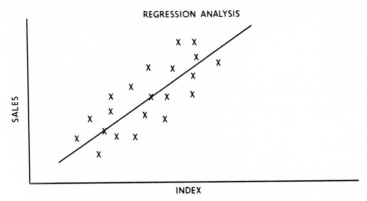

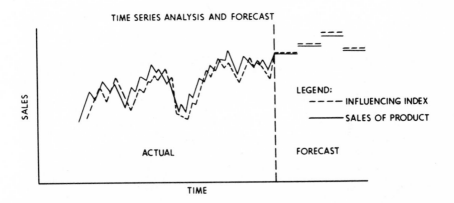

Linear allocation model. The allocation model is generally defined as the most efficient allocation of limited resources to competing requirements. The problem can be represented geometrically if there are three or fewer competing requirements; beyond this it must be solved by the use of matrix algebra, frequently described as the "Simplex method." This is a procedure which through a series of repetitive operations (iterations) progressively approaches and ultimately reaches an optimum solution. It has been applied to a wide variety of allocation problems—including product mix determination, ingredient blending, capacity allocation, purchasing and evaluation of bids, and distribution.

Figure 4 illustrates the following distribution problem: Assign the production of three plants to fill the sales requirements of four warehouses at the minimum shipping costs.[11] Let us assume, as *known,* the

[11]A similar but more complex distribution problem is developed by Edward H. Bowman and John B. Stewart in "A Model for Scale of Operations," *Journal of Marketing,* Vol. 20 (January, 1956), pp. 242–47.

FIGURE 4

RESOURCE ALLOCATION PROBLEM

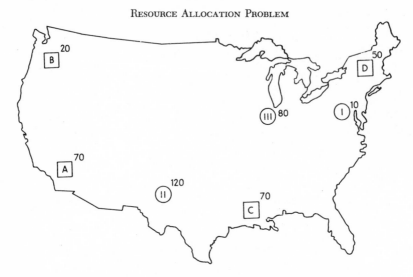

Problem: Assign production of three plants to fill requirements
of four warehouses at the minimum shipping cost.

requirements of each warehouse, the capacity of each plant, and the
shipping cost from each plant to each warehouse. For simplification,
total productive capacity is considered equal to total sales requirements. The map illustrates the relative locations of plants and warehouses, and the matrix developed in Table 1 shows all of the known
data.

TABLE 1

FREIGHT RATES
Production = Demand = 210 Units

Factory → Warehouse	I	II	III	Production → Demand
	10	120	80	
A	1.05	.90	2.00	70
B	2.30	1.40	1.40	20
C	1.80	1.00	1.20	70
D	1.00	1.75	1.10	50

The following steps (the Simplex method) lead to the solution of this problem, shown in Figure 5 and in Table 2:

1. Frame the problem, stating all requirements.
2. Determine an initial solution.
3. Evaluate the various choices.
4. Select the most favorable choice.
5. Determine the number and distribution of units reallocated.
6. Develop the new solution.
7. Repeat steps 3 through 6 until no possible favorable choices are available.
   At this point the procedure is complete. There can be no better solution.

FIGURE 5

SOLUTION TO RESOURCE ALLOCATION PROBLEM

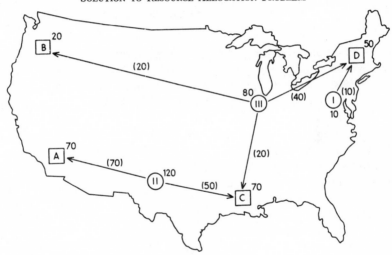

TABLE 2

OPTIMUM PRODUCTION DISTRIBUTION

Solution	I	II	III	Demand
A		70		70
B			20	20
C		50	20	70
D	10		40	50
Prod.	10	120	80	

Nonlinear allocation model. There is no single methodology for the solution of nonlinear allocation problems. Many lend themselves to simulation, Monte Carlo analysis, or queuing theory. Some, however, can be solved by linear programming if they exhibit nonlinear relationships which can be approximated by straight lines (or planes), or nonlinear relationships which can be reduced to linearity.

Dynamic allocation model. As noted, dynamic allocation models frequently are solved by making optimum decisions for each step and proceeding from one stage to the next, integrating these interim solutions in following stages. A final optimum solution is achieved by summing each of the interim solutions.

PROVED APPLICATIONS

The number of business problems to which O.R. has been successfully applied is far greater than the marketing problems discussed, as the following list shows:

1. Selection of advertising media and expenditures.
2. Revision of price and discount tables.
3. Establishment of bonus and incentive plans.
4. Strategy moves in view of competitive conditions.
5. Sales forecasting.
6. Sales (customer) service policies.
7. Sales effort management.
8. Product (inventory) distribution.
9. Selection of warehouse location.
10. Inventory policies.
11. Formulation of new product plans.
12. Research budget allocations.
13. Determination of product mix.
14. Transportation mix.
15. Distribution scheduling.

The principal objective of this article has been to create an awareness of a powerful new tool, its concepts, approaches to problem solving, and the techniques by which it translates ideas into decisions. Properly applied, O.R. will enable business to cope more effectively with its problems, and to meet the increasingly complex and demanding responsibilities with which it is faced.

12. MODELING OF MARKET AND COMPANY INTERACTIONS*

Jay W. Forrester

All of you in marketing recognize that many linkages connect a company to its market. Some of these linkages are tangible like the flow of orders toward the company and the counterflow of product to the customer. Other linkages are obvious like the sales efforts and advertising expended to communicate with the market. But many linkages are subtle and tenuous like those that carry customer attitudes and needs back to the decision-making points in the company.

But recognizing these linkages between company and market does not mean that one can see clearly the time-varying responses caused by interactions between them. It is in the interplay of forces caused by these interacting linkages that we find the causes of company and product growth and conversely find the influences which can cause stagnation and decline.

These company-market linkages form networks of feedback loops. In these loops an action by the company causes a response in the market which in turn produces the information on which decisions are based to control future company actions. The dynamic behavior of these feedback loops is poorly understood and contains many surprises.

The complexity of these interactions is far too great for analytical solution using conventional mathematical approaches. With trivial exceptions, mathematics deals only with linear systems. Yet some of the most important behavior mechanisms in marketing depend for their very existence on nonlinear relationships. The only effective tool for understanding nonlinear, multiple-loop feedback systems is the construction of a model that permits simulation of the behavior relationships which we perceive within the company and market.

The construction of models to represent market dynamics is now possible. The problem is not, as often supposed, the need for more empirical data. The pace of progress will be set entirely by the availability of investigators who understand the kinds of factors that are important in feedback system behavior and who can conceptually structure the presently available information and data.

Some of the linkages between a company and market appear in Figure 1. The company uses incoming information from the market as the basis for generating the outputs from company to market. These outputs gen-

---

*From *Marketing and Economic Development,* American Marketing Association, September, 1965, pp. 353–64.

erated by the company include price and the quality of products and services. Another output from the company is delivery delay which reflects the relationship between incoming order rate and production capability. Product suitability reflects the adequacy of new product development and the degree of perception by the company of market needs. Sales effort is a result of the company's resource allocation policies.

FIGURE 1

COMPANY-MARKET LINKAGES

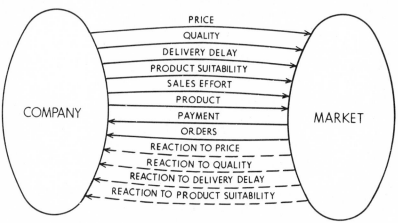

In the opposite direction from market to company, there is, of course, a flow of orders and payments. But there are also other important information streams. These might be defined in a variety of ways. One useful structuring of information from the market to the company is in terms of reflections of those linkages which the company projects to the market. The company should be interested in the market reactions toward price, quality, delivery delay, and product suitability.

Starting from Figure 1, to construct a dynamic simulation model requires that we define the responses that we believe exist in the two separate sectors—the company and the market. In each sector the task is to take the incoming inputs as a basis for generating the outputs. Within the company the time delays and policy interactions must be represented which convert market information into the outputs of price, quality, delivery delay, product suitability, sales effort, and product flow. Within the market the characteristics must be conceptualized and defined which we believe react to the inputs from the company and generate a stream of orders as well as the sources of information flowing to the company. This means that the model represents our operational knowledge about the management processes in the company and the customer processes in the market.

Figure 1 implies the futility of attempting to teach marketing as an isolated corporate function. In the corporation, marketing shares with the area of management information systems the characteristic that it depends on an unusually high number of linkages to other parts of the business system. It is not self-sufficient. By contrast, production is a more self-contained corporate function. I feel that this high degree of inter-connectedness in marketing explains many of the difficulties encountered in attempting to teach the subject. Marketing can not be successfully isolated from its dynamic interactions with other company functions.

In Figure 1 we see implied many of the simpler feedback loops in the system. Company activities to generate quality lead to an actual product quality that produces a market reaction to quality and an information return to the company about the reaction to quality which is one of the inputs to the future management of quality. Likewise, a loop connects company price policy through prices to the market and back through the reaction of the market to price. But the system is not a collection of separate and isolated loops controlling the separate company outputs. There are many important cross couplings. For example, a policy which reduces price can reduce the payment stream and thereby company profits so that pressure is brought on the activities controlling quality which then may lower the quality output from the company and in time cause a decrease in market orders. The feedback loops connecting company and market have many devious interconnections. The dynamic interactions within these loops can defeat our attempts at intuitive judgment about system behavior.

Some of the feedback loops between company and market are so-called "negative feedback loops" which attempt to adjust system operation toward some reference goal. Other loops are "positive feedback" in character and these latter account for the processes of growth and decline.

FIGURE 2

POSITIVE FEEDBACK IN SALES GROWTH

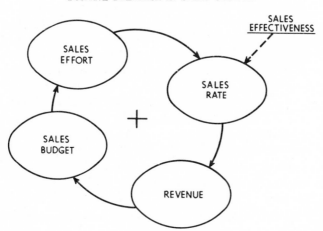

Figure 2 shows an example of a positive feedback loop involved in the growth of a new product. The sales effort operating at some sales effectiveness produces a sales rate. The sales effectiveness is a reflection of the desirability of the product and is a measure of the ease with which it can be sold. The sales rate generates revenue. A part of the revenue becomes available in the sales budget to support future sales effort. If the sales effectiveness is high enough and the fraction of revenue going to the sales budget is large enough, then a given sales effort will produce a sales rate and budget higher than necessary to sustain the initial sales effort. Under these favorable circumstances, sales effort leads to a growing sales budget which then supports an increasing sales effort. The regenerative growth process continues until something within the loop, perhaps the sales effectiveness, changes in an unfavorable direction. The rapidity of growth depends on the coefficients in the system such as the sales effectiveness and the fraction of revenue going to the support of sales effort. The rapidity of growth is also directly influenced by the delays around the loop. Because of the market delays, the sales rate lags behind the corresponding sales effort; because of manufacturing and invoice collection delays, the revenue lags behind the sales rate; because of the corporate budgeting procedures, the sales budget lags behind the incoming revenue; and because of the time to locate and train salesmen, the sales effort lags behind the budget. Other conditions being equal, the rate of sales growth will be doubled if the delays around this positive feedback loop can be reduced to half.

Conversely, a positive feedback loop can show degenerative decline. In the example of Figure 2, if the sales effectiveness is low, the sales effort may not support its own sales budget leading to a future reduction in sales effort that further reduces sales. Positive feedback loops can exhibit either growth or decay. By contrast, negative feedback loops tend to adjust activity toward a reference goal but in the attempt they often produce fluctuation.

Figure 3 shows a negative feedback loop coupling sales rate, order backlog, delivery delay, and sales effectiveness. In this diagram it is assumed that sales effort remains constant. The relationship between order backlog and sales rate depends on the production capacity characteristics of the company. For illustration, assume that the production capacity is constant and the sales effort is more than adequate to create the corresponding sales rate if delivery delay is short. Under these circumstances, sales rate will exceed production capacity and the order backlog will increase. The increase in the order backlog will continue until the resulting increase in delivery delay becames sufficient that some customers become unwilling to wait for delivery. As the delivery delay becomes longer, the product becomes less attractive and the product becomes less easy to sell. This means that, as delivery delay increases, the sales effectiveness declines until sales rate falls to the production

FIGURE 3

<small>NEGATIVE FEEDBACK LIMITING SALES</small>

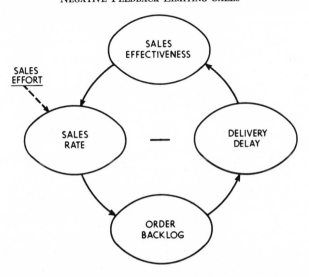

capability. This negative feedback loop is at work in any market situation where delivery delays are long enough to be of concern to the customer. A negative feedback loop as shown in Figure 3 can exhibit instability. There are delays at each point in the loop. The sales rate does not respond immediately to changes in delivery delay because many of the orders under negotiation are already committed and cannot be redirected. Order backlog is an accumulation over time of discrepancies between the sales rate and the production capacity and backlog lags behind a change in sales rate. Delivery delay here represents the delay recognized by the market and this lags behind the true delay as indicated by the order backlog. These delays, coupled with the other characteristics of the loop, can lead to overcorrection. A sales rate which is too high goes unrecognized until the backlog builds up and until the delivery delay is recognized. By this time delivery delay is excessive and leads to a reduction in sales rate below the production capacity. Then, order backlog declines unduly before the low delivery delay is recognized and sales again rise.

An important part of the negative feedback loop of Figure 3 is the nonlinear relationship between delivery delay and sales effectiveness as shown in Figure 4. Sales effectiveness is a maximum when delivery is zero. For very small delivery delays (measured in seconds for a drugstore item and up to months for a digital computer) there is no reduction of sales as delivery delay increases. However, with longer delivery delays, a region of steep slope is encountered where the delay is sufficient to discourage a progressively larger fraction of customers. For still longer delays, the curve levels out as it approaches zero sales effectiveness,

FIGURE 4

NONLINEAR RELATIONSHIP

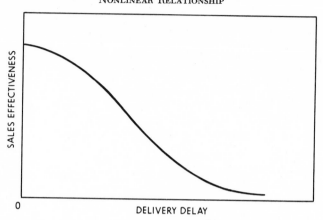

representing the fact that a few customers find the product particularly suitable and are willing to plan ahead and wait unusually long.

Now what would happen in a coupled company and market system involving the two control loops of Figures 2 and 3? These are shown interconnected in Figure 5. Here, if we assume that only a limited production capacity is available, the positive feedback loop will regenerate a rising rate of sales until the production capacity limit is reached. When the production rate no longer increases with sales, the negative loop would show an increasing delivery delay and this would produce a declining sales effectiveness to limit further growth. This process of growth limitation is commonly encountered in many subtle ways in new product situations. A new product may enjoy adequate production as long as it does not encroach seriously on established products. As the new product grows, it may find increasing difficulty in competing for available capacity. Capacity limitation is often not recognized because its effect can occur even before the plant facilities are operating at maximum output. As the plant begins to reach its full capacity, flexibility is lost and orders for special variations in the product cause congestion and confusion. Average delivery delay increases even though it appears that the manufacturing capacity is still not fully occupied. Any situation where order backlogs are long enough to be viewed unfavorably by customers implies that this negative feedback loop is active in partially suppressing sales. Figure 5 can be recognized as an extremely simplified subset of the possible interactions contained in Figure 1. Even in this severely simplified form of Figure 5, the implied system behavior cannot be intuitively estimated as one contemplates changing the many factors within the two coupled loops.

The growth behavior of the double-loop system under one set of system

FIGURE 5

COUPLED NEGATIVE AND POSITIVE FEEDBACK LOOPS

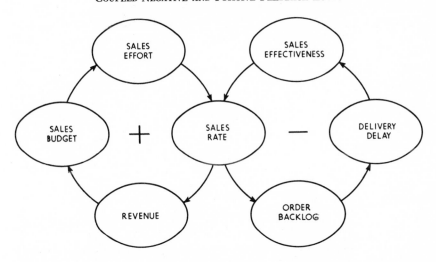

conditions is shown in Figure 6. The figure is taken from a simulation run using "industrial dynamics" methods[1] and the DYNAMO compiler[2] for simulating the model. Growth in sales rate occurs during the first 60 months. Thereafter sales tend to fluctuate because the production capacity limit has been reached. During the early period of growth, sales effectiveness remains constant and high while at the same time the delivery delay remains constant and low. As the sales rate begins to approach the production capacity, the delivery delay increases and the sales effectiveness falls. After month 60, the system fluctuates because of the characteristics of the negative feedback loop in which readjustments within the loop are delayed and instability occurs on either side of the equilibrium position.

The major characteristics of Figure 6—the rapidity of early growth and the fluctuation during the stagnation period—depend on the parameters and the time delays in the two loops. The positive feedback loop of Figure 2 is the primary determinant of the growth phase shown in Figure 6; and the negative feedback loop in Figure 3 is the primary determinant of the behavior after sales growth has been arrested by reaching the production capacity. In Figure 6 we see a transition from positive feedback loop behavior to negative loop behavior which is triggered by the nonlinear characteristics represented in the production capacity and the sales effectiveness.

In Figures 5 and 6, the cessation of sales growth could not be fore-

[1]J. W. Forrester, *Industrial Dynamics* (Cambridge, Mass.: M.I.T. Press, 1961).
[2]A. L. Pugh, III, *DYNAMO User's Manual*, 2d ed. (Cambridge, Mass.: M.I.T. Press, 1963).

FIGURE 6

GROWTH AND STAGNATION IN SALES

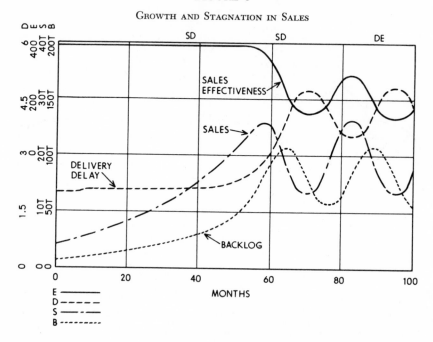

stalled by improved or expanded marketing activities. A larger fraction of revenue devoted to sales effort would only cause the delivery delay to increase further and drive down the sales effectiveness to still lower values. Similar interactions, within the multiple channels of the far greater complexity of real-life situations, can invalidate marketing decisions by the inner workings of the market-company system.

It is sufficient to say that any marketing decision considered by itself is apt to become a victim of other interacting factors.

When one examines a model of the interactions between company and market, he discovers many mechanisms which can cause limitation in sales and stagnation in growth. In fact, one should reverse the common query, "How can I increase sales?" A better question is "How should one limit sales?" It is clear that one must limit sales. If the product has the highest quality, immediate delivery, the most suitable design, the widest distribution, the best salesmen, and the lowest price, sales will exceed the physical or financial capability of the company.

The oversimplified economic view suggests that price is the mechanism which balances supply and demand. But as a practical matter this is not true. There is no way to determine a price which will cause exact balance between supply and demand. Price is established on the basis of manufacturing cost, past traditions, competitors' prices, or in response to financial pressures on the company. If the price is set lower than the economic equilibrium value, then other influences must share the burden of limiting orders. The first effect will usually be a rise in delivery delay to make the product less attractive. After a period of long deliveries, the company may grow careless and allow quality to decline so that the lower quality contributes to limiting sales. The company profitability is, however, very sensitive to the balance of factors at work in the limitation of sales. As more of the burden is shifted to long delivery delay, lower quality, obsolete design, and unskilled salesmen, the price must be correspondingly lowered to maintain sales. Profit margins fall and create financial pressures which cause further deterioration in the product characteristics of interest to the customer. A degenerative spiral can then develop with lower quality forcing lower prices which exert financial pressure and further reduce quality.

Returning to Figure 1 we see a number of information channels flowing from market to company carrying information about market reactions to company performance. These information channels are of the utmost importance in determining the kinds of decisions made within the company. Yet these information channels are subject to many ills. The quality of an information channel can be measured in several ways—by its persuasiveness, delay, bias, distortion, error, and cross talk.

An information channel usually shows greater persuasiveness and influence on the decision-making processes as it deals with short-term factors and as it deals with information which is easily measured. Information is more persuasive when the method of measurement is well known and widely accepted. For example, inventory information is highly persuasive since it appears monthly on the balance sheet measured to five decimal places (even though it may not be truly meaningful even in the first decimal place). By contrast, information indicating what the customers think of the company's product quality lacks persuasiveness because it is difficult to measure and hard to define. Oftentimes the most important information is the least persuasive.

Delay represents the time it takes information to travel along a channel. Information delays can be very long. For example, there can easily be a five-year delay between the quality actually produced in a product and the reputation for quality which is prevalent in the market. The time taken to judge quality is partly controlled by the natural life of the product. A meaningful measure of quality in an electric refrigerator can only be made if one waits through the normal life of the refrigerator. Even after quality is observed directly by a user, further delays are encountered before this reputation is transmitted to potential customers who have not been users.

Bias is the offset in an information channel where the perceived information deviates consistently from the true conditions. One often sees bias in a company's belief about the degree to which customers are satisfied. The company wants to believe it is doing well. Favorable reports bolster the self image and are remembered and circulated. Unfavorable reports are dismissed as exceptions or as unfortunate accidents.

Distortion is a deviation between the input and output of an information channel which is a function of the nature of the information itself. Distortion is sometimes intentional as in an averaging process. Averaging of sales data suppresses short-term fluctuation while allowing longer term deviations to be transmitted. The fidelity of the process therefore depends on the periodicity of the information being transmitted.

Error refers to random deviations and mistakes in an information channel. More effort is expended in reducing error than in reducing any of the other types of information deficiencies. Yet of the six types of information degradation, error is probably least important in affecting the feedback systems that couple a company to its market.

Cross talk is a term borrowed from telephone usage and represents the tendency of information to be transposed from one channel to another. Transposition of the meaning of information is conspicuously evident in the channels flowing from market to company. There is a tendency for all customer dissatisfaction to take the form of indicating that the price is too high. This can happen at many points in the information channels. Price is too high for the low quality, or price is too high for the poor delivery, or price is too high for the discourteous salesmen. But the qualification is lost and only the reference to price is transmitted. Suppose that the customer is dissatisfied with the performance of his last purchase. He has decided not to buy again. When the salesman appears, the socially acceptable and most expeditious reason for not buying is to say that the price is too high. That is value judgment which the salesman cannot effectively counter. Were the customer to complain of quality, the salesman might offer to send a service engineer or he might explain how quality control at the factory has been improved. Or he might offer to take back the equipment for repair. But, if the customer wants none of these and wants not to be bothered, he says the price is too high. Suppose, however, that the customer does complain about the low quality and the obsolete design. Will the salesman risk the wrath of the development department and the factory by carrying these complaints back to the home plant? Probably not. He will simply report that the price is too high. But suppose that the salesman has courage to press complaints of an obsolete product. What will the management do to restore falling sales? It may well reduce price because it knows how to accomplish that, whereas a redesign is uncertain and far in the future.

From simulation of the information channels and decision-making policies that create the company-market system one can learn much about the behavior which in real life is so baffling. Interactions are complex. The human mind is not well adapted to intuitively estimating the behavior of complex feedback linkages. Marketing is a function which cannot exist by itself. It is intimately coupled to production, capital investment policies, product design, and the company's educational programs. As one makes changes in a particular set of market linkages he may simply create greater difficulties in another area. It is only through knowledge of the entire system that successful coupling between company and market can be achieved.

13. THE ACCELERATION EFFECT IN FORECASTING INDUSTRIAL SHIPMENTS*

Alfred A. Kuehn and Ralph L. Day

While simple extrapolative techniques are frequently useful, real progress in the art of industrial sales forecasting is more likely to result from an effort to understand the behavior of business firms and fit relevant patterns of business behavior into a useful framework of analysis.

The method of analysis presented here considers typical levels of inventory, in the hands of the various types of middlemen and users, as the relevant pattern of behavior and employs the acceleration principle as the unifying framework for analysis.

This approach to the forecasting problem was developed during three years of work in forecasting factory shipments of a specialty steel product. It has resulted in improved forecasts and a better understanding of the process of distribution in this segment of industry; and it seems to hold promise for more general application.

THE ACCELERATION PRINCIPLE

The idea that holders of inventories tend to maintain inventory levels in a constant ratio to sales, thus amplifying the magnitude of changes in their orders on suppliers, is generally known as the "acceleration effect." The acceleration principle has been treated frequently in the literature of economics; and a number of empirical studies have attempted to measure the effect of acceleration on the overall level of inventory investment.[1] These studies have generally dealt with highly aggregated data, lumping together many industries and many forms of inventory.

The study of aggregative inventory data has tended to confirm that

*Journal of Marketing, January, 1963, pp. 25–28.

[1] Lloyd A. Metzler, "The Nature and Stability of Inventory Cycles," *Review of Economics and Statistics*, Vol. 23 (August, 1941), pp. 113–29. Also: Paul G. Darling, "Manufacturers' Inventory Investment 1947–58: An Application of Accelerator Analysis," *American Economic Review*, Vol. 49 (December, 1959), pp. 950–62; Moses Abramovitz, *Inventories and Business Cycles, with Special Reference to Manufacturers Inventories* (New York: National Bureau of Economic Research, 1950); Michael Lovell, "Manufacturers Inventories, Sales Expectations, and the Acceleration Principle," *Econometrica*, Vol. 29 (July, 1961), pp. 293–314.

the accelerator principle does operate. However, researchers have concluded that the full effect of the accelerator is typically not achieved.[2] That is, adjustments take place in the direction which the accelerator indicates, but the constant ratio to sales is not completely achieved. Suggested explanations have ranged from the idea that businessmen strive only for a partial adjustment to the desired levels of inventory in a given period to the hypothesis that errors in sales forecasting cause discrepancies between actual and desired levels of inventories.[3]

Many possible explanations of the statistical results could lie buried in the highly aggregated dollar volume inventory data which have been used by economic researchers. In any event, the failure of inventory data of broad segments of industry to show the full achievement of the accelerator effect does not seriously challenge the suitability of the acceleration principle for the analysis of inventory behavior in a particular industry. Results in the tool steel case presented below tend to confirm its usefulness in such a context.

A HYPOTHETICAL CASE

The implications of the acceleration principle for industrial forecasting can be illustrated by a hypothetical example. The forecaster for a firm producing a special-purpose alloy wishes to forecast total factory shipments by all manufacturers of the alloy during the coming year. Careful analysis of all available data—including forecasts by trade associations, financial institutions, and government agencies—indicates that activity of consuming industries in the coming period will be up approximately 20 percent from the present level. The forecaster finds no discernible trends in the pattern of use of the product or any other indications that the industry's participation in the rising market will be atypical. The forecaster conducts a sample survey which establishes that current inventory levels of middlemen and final users are normal and that users' expectations are consistent with the estimated 20 percent rise in activity. On the basis of these data, he predicts that factory shipments will be up 20 percent over the previous period.

One year later it appears that consumption of the product was up during the year by almost exactly 20 percent. But this is little consolation to the forecaster. Factory shipments were up not 20 percent but 33 percent, even though inventory levels were normal at the beginning and end of the period. The explanation of the discrepancy is simple once

[2]Michael Lovell, *loc. cit.*, p. 293.

[3]For the first view, see Richard M. Goodwin, "Secular and Cyclical Aspects of the Multiplier and Accelerator," *Income Employment and Public Policy: Essays in Honor of Alvin H. Hansen* (New York: Norton and Co., 1948). For the second view, see Lloyd A. Metzler, "The Nature and Stability of Inventory Cycles," *Review of Economics and Statistics,* Vol. 23 (August, 1941), pp. 113–29.

inventory behavior of final users and intermediaries is carefully examined.

In this hypothetical industry the manufacturers sell to fabricators who maintain their inventory levels at a nine-weeks' supply. The fabricators sell to jobbers who maintain a 15-weeks' supply. Jobbers in turn sell to the final industrial consumers who maintain a five-weeks' supply.

When the ultimate user's sales increase 20 percent, he must increase purchases by 21.9 percent in order to maintain his normal five-weeks' supply at the new level of sales $[20\% + 20\%(5/52)] = 20\%[1 + .2(.096)] = 21.9\%]$. Jobbers now have a 21.9 percent increase in sales. To maintain the normal 15-weeks' supply at this new level of sales, jobbers purchase at a rate of 128.2 percent of the previous period's sales $[21.9\% + 21.9\%(15/52)] = 21.9\%[1 + 21.9(.288)] = 28.2\%)$. To meet the 128.2 percent rate of sales and maintain their 9-weeks' supply of inventory, the fabricators must now buy from manufacturers at a rate of 133.1 percent of the previous period's purchases.

Thus, a 20 percent increase in demand by final users resulted in a 33 percent increase in factory shipments, although industrial consumers and middlemen maintained their inventories at "normal" levels based on a standard time period of supply. Failure to anticipate the inventory adjustments necessary to maintain customary inventory relationships led to a sizable underestimation of factory shipments. A drop in demand would lead to adjustments in the opposite direction and result in overestimation of factory shipments if the accelerator effect were not recognized.

ANALYZING INVENTORY BEHAVIOR

The cumulative effects, at the various stages of distribution, of acceleration of changes in demand is very useful in explaining the relatively violent fluctuations in factory shipments in many industries.

However, the accelerator cannot be mechanically applied to predicted changes in final consumption. Perfect adjustment to the standard time period of supply at all stages in the distributive system at any point in time is quite unlikely. The application of the accelerator effect as a forecasting tool is advisable only after careful study of inventory behavior at all points in the distribution channels through which the product reaches the final user. Undetected changes in the standard time period of supply or temporary deviations from the standard at the beginning of a forecast period can result in substantial forecasting errors. Adjusting for changes of this nature is not a serious problem unless inventory levels are inherently unstable and unpredictable.

Although inventory levels in any industry are subject to variations, many firms establish a standard or target inventory level stated as a given number of weeks' supply at the current demand level. The stan-

FIGURE 1

DISTRIBUTION FLOW DIAGRAM: HYPOTHETICAL METALS INDUSTRY

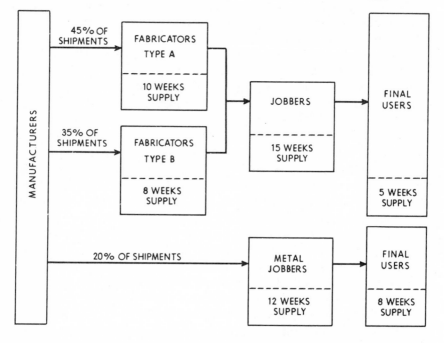

dard inventory level is determined by many factors, including lead times from suppliers, delivery time required by customers, and the costs of holding inventory. The standard number of weeks' supply varies among industries and varies within industries according to the nature of the firm, its immediate suppliers, and its customers.

The first step in preparing to use the acceleration principle as a forecasting tool is to identify different classes of consumers and intermediate purchasers in the industry according to their role in the industry and according to patterns of inventory behavior. It is helpful to prepare a diagram or flow chart for the industry which indicates the various paths the basic product takes in reaching the final consumer, the relative importance of each path, and the normal inventory position at each point in the distributive network.

A flow chart for a hypothetical metal product is given in Figure 1. Manufacturers ship to three classes of customers—two types of fabricators and metal jobbers. The fabricators perform manufacturing operations on the basic metal product, but it remains in separate and identifiable form. The fabricators sell to jobbers who in turn sell to final consumers. The metal jobbers do not alter the product but sell it in its original form to industrial consumers. The relative importance of each class of the manufacturers' customers can be computed from historical data and can be updated each forecasting period. The normal time period of supply at each point in the distribution network can be determined by a sample survey of the various types of inventory holders or through some form of continuing reporting service.[4] Determination of the existing levels of inventory at the beginning of each forecast period then becomes a part of the forecasting procedure.

Once the structural pattern of the industry and the standard time period of supply at each point have been determined, the basic structure for forecasting factory shipments from projections of final consumption is established. The acceleration effect can be computed from the consumer back through the intermediate purchasers to the manufacturers of the basic product for each of the channels.

The results are then weighted by the percentage of factory shipments going to each segment of the industry to determine the expected level of factory shipments. However, this can be done only after the actual levels of inventory at the beginning of a period are checked against the standard levels. If deviations are of small magnitude and appear to be of a random nature, they can be ignored. If discrepancies between actual levels and standard levels are large or if these discrepancies occur in some discernible pattern, then adjustments must be made.

If discrepancies at the beginning of the period are large but there is no reason to believe that abnormal levels will persist during the coming period, discrepancies can easily be handled as adjustments within the accelerator framework. Suppose in the hypothetical example above that a strike threat at the fabricator level had caused jobbers to increase inventory levels to a 19-weeks' supply instead of the standard 15-weeks' supply, but that the strike threat had passed. The extra four weeks' inventory will dampen the effect of the new level of user demand. The extra inventory holdings amount to 7.7 percent of the previous year's demand. Therefore, jobbers' demand will be at a level of 120.5 percent of the previous year's level, instead of the 128.2 percent level which would have held if jobbers' inventories had been normal.

If deviations from the normal time period of supply at any point in the distributive network do not appear to be of a transitory nature, such as those caused by strike scares or price speculation, then it becomes necessary to predict what the inventory holding will be during the forecast period.

Methods for establishing an inventory level to be used in the accelerator model can vary from personal judgments made by the forecaster (because of his general knowledge of the circumstances) to sophisticated models of inventory behavior established for each class of firm in the distribution network. The particular approach to be used depends

---

[4]For a description of a telegraphic reporting service, see John Parkany, "A New Approach to Sales Forecasting and Production Scheduling," *Journal of Marketing*, Vol. 25 (January, 1961), pp. 14–21.

on the importance of the forecast and the skills and inclinations of the forecaster. Experience suggests that if the industry structure is analyzed to the point that a meaningful flow diagram can be constructed and maintained, reasons for changes in the inventory levels of particular classes of consumers and middlemen are generally apparent and adjustments can be made on a judgmental basis.

A promising approach is to study the behavior of the various types of firms in the industry structure, with a view to developing simple decision rules or "rules of thumb" which explain their reactions to various observable phenomena with particular respect to inventory behavior. This approach logically culminates in a computer simulation of the industry which incorporates the structural representation of the industry such as is suggested in Figure 1, the decision rules of the various classes of middlemen and industrial consumers, and the accelerator principle.[5]

A CASE IN POINT: TOOL STEEL

Graphic evidence of the operation of the accelerator effect can be seen in Figure 2, which shows factory shipments of tool steel for the 10-year period 1948–57, in comparison with an index of metal working activity and an estimate of tool steel consumption.

The "Metalworking Index" was originally developed in an attempt to establish a long-term history of tool steel consumption. It is a weighted composite of relevant Federal Reserve Board indices. In the period 1949–57, it increasingly overestimated tool steel consumption, as carbide cutting tools and dies replaced tool steel in some industrial applications. This is reflected in the graph of "Estimated Tool Steel Consumption" which is based on the Metalworking Index, adjusted for increases in consumption of carbides.

The relatively erratic movements of factory shipments can be explained in large part by the accelerator effect when inventory positions at the beginning of the year are related to the normal time period of supply. The downturn in demand in 1949 from 1948 was reflected in an accelerated manner, as was the upturn of 1950. The "normal" acceleration was exaggerated in 1951 due to an inventory buildup beyond the usual time period of supply as a result of influences of the Korean War, particularly price speculation. When the rate of increase in demand leveled off in 1952 and 1953, liquidations of excess inventory were great enough to cause the level of shipments to drop even though the absolute level of demand was still rising. Inventories were more nearly "balanced" in the years 1954–57; and tool steel shipments reflected the movements in consumption in a highly accelerated fashion, rising and

---

[5]For a description of a computer simulation involving inventories, see Jay W. Forrester, *Industrial Dynamics* (New York: John Wiley & Sons, 1961), particularly chap. 15.

FIGURE 2

FACTORY SHIPMENTS OF TOOL STEEL COMPARED WITH ESTIMATES OF CONSUMPTION

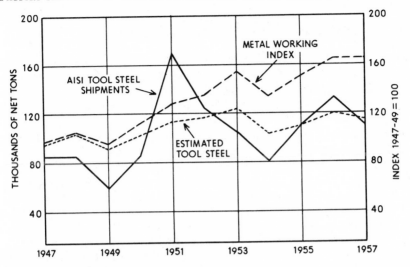

dropping at much faster rates than the corresponding changes in usage of the product by industry.

SUMMARY

When reasonably accurate forecasts of final consumption can be made, the accelerator effect coupled with a continuing study of patterns of inventory behavior can provide a very useful approach to forecasting factory shipments of basic industrial products.

No attempt has been made here to outline a forecasting procedure which can be directly applied to any industry; but a reorientation of thinking about the forecasting problem has been suggested. Emphasis is shifted from a search for mechanical statistical relationships to a quest for understanding of the behavior of the many types of firms which make up an industry structure and the way in which the operations of these firms interact to influence manufacturers sales.

If used uncritically as another mechanical relationship, the acceleration model can produce poorer results than the usual statistical approaches to forecasting. If the direction of movements in final consumption of a product is incorrectly forecast, the error could be amplified by the acceleration effect. If inventory behavior is grossly misinterpreted, further errors can result.

But the possibilities of misuse do not deny the promise of this approach—a better understanding of the way in which elements of the distributive framework of an industry react to changes in the consumption of the product.

Suggested additional AMA readings

Amstutz, Arnold, and Tallman, Gerald B. "Dynamic Simulation Applied to Marketing," in *Marketing Keys to Profits in the 1960's*, pp. 78–95. Chicago: American Marketing Association, 1959.

Bowman, Edward N., and Stewart, John B. "A Model for Scale Operations," *Journal of Marketing*, July, 1965, pp. 242–47.

Buzzell, Robert D. *A Basic Bibliography on Mathematical Methods in Marketing*. Chicago: American Marketing Association, 1962.

Gauthier, Howard L. "Potential for the Use of Graph Theory in Logistics System Evolution," in *Science, Technology, and Marketing*, pp. 359–70. Chicago: American Marketing Association, Fall Conference Proceedings, 1966.

Maffei, Richard B. "Modern Methods for Local Delivery Route Design," *Journal of Marketing*, July, 1965, pp. 13–18.

Massey, William F., and Sannas, Jim D. "Logical Flow Models for Marketing Analysis," *Journal of Marketing*, July, 1964, pp. 30–37.

McGee, John F. "Operations Research in Making Marketing Decisions," *Journal of Marketing*, October, 1960, pp. 18–23.

McLaughlin, Robert L. *Time Series Forecasting*. Chicago: American Marketing Association, 1964.

Whiteman, Irvin R. "New Reasoning in Choosing a Warehouse Location," *Journal of Marketing*, January, 1964, pp. 38–43.

Part III

LOGISTICS OF DISTRIBUTION CHANNELS

As suggested in the preface, distribution channel structure and logistics performance are inherently tied together. The nature and number of channel intermediaries, as well as the marketing services and inventory practices, affect the logistics task. The method of processing orders, transportation and storage, and matching production with demand in turn affect the marketing channel and its performance.

In this section, two articles provide an overview of the logistics-channel relationship. Bowersox (14) discusses changes in channel structures resulting from scrambled merchandising and examines several problems of a channel structure–logistics performance nature. Bucklin (15) proposes a theory of channel organization and the organization of inventories within the channel. Emphasis is on the concept of postponement: differentiating products as near to the customer as possible, and speculation: producing in anticipation of sale. These two concepts are combined to yield six hypotheses concerning channel structure.

14. CHANGING CHANNELS IN THE PHYSICAL DISTRIBUTION OF FINISHED GOODS*

Donald J. Bowersox

Today, retailers sell wholesale, wholesalers sell retail, hardware stores sell soft goods, department stores sell food, food stores sell appliances, they all sell toys, and discount stores sell everything. Channel jumping is not limited to retailing. Finished goods often move to the same retailer from wholesalers, distributors, jobbers, assemblers, and direct from producers. In some cases, goods bypass the retailer altogether moving directly to

*From *Marketing and Economic Development,* American Marketing Association, September, 1965, pp. 711–21.

consumers. In short, traditional classifications of middlemen, trade channels, and goods have lost considerable validity.

The cost pressures of scrambled marketing have forced a careful review of physical distribution practices. While "you can't do busines from an empty wagon," the yardstick of how you replenish the wagon may mean the difference between profit or loss.[1] Physical distribution is recognized as the management responsibility to design and administer systems for controlling raw material and finished inventory replenishment.[2] Case studies of firms who have improved physical distribution efficiency are widely publicized in business and trade journals.[3] This spurt of attention to physical flow has resulted from sheer magnitude of expenditure and the relatively untapped opportunities for cost reduction.

Many corporate costs of replenishment are hidden between traditional departments of an enterprise and not necessarily under the control of any given department. In addition, the actions of any single department may reduce that department's share of expenditure while at the same time increase total corporate cost of physical distribution.[4] It takes a major revision in management philosophy to achieve interdepartmental control over physical distribution costs.

Little consideration has been given to the problems of coordinating or controlling physical distribution beyond the legal boundaries of individual firms.[5] Most physical distribution flow proceeds from production to consumption through a variety of specialized enterprise units linked together as a distribution channel. Each of these independent units may perform an excellent individual job of physical distribution while simultaneously the channel as a group suffers from expensive duplication.

The entire notion of loosely aligned middlemen seems to condemn

[1]Adopted from feature article "Distribution—Growth Pattern for Tomorrow," *Annual Report of Dun and Bradstreet, Inc.,* 1964.

[2]For expansion see: Donald J. Bowersox, "The Role of the Marketing Executive in Physical Distribution," in George L. Baker (ed.), *Effective Marketing Coordination, Proceedings American Marketing Association* (Chicago: American Marketing Association, 1961), pp. 393-99.

[3]For examples see: H. Jay Bullen, "New Competitive Selling Weapon—Physical Distribution Management," *Sales Management,* May, 1965, pp. 41-52; "The Next Place For Paring Costs," *Business Week,* May 1, 1965; Joel F. Olesky, "Distribution Comes of Age," *Dun's Review,* January, 1965, pp. 36-38; and John R. Staley, "Nineteen Ways to Save Time and Money in Distribution," *Business Management,* September, 1964, pp. 42-46.

[4]Physical distribution applications of the total cost concept are explained in: Howard T. Lewis, James W. Culliton, and Jack D. Steel, *The Role of Air Freight In Physical Distribution* (Boston: Division of Research, Graduate School of Business Administration, Harvard University, 1956), and Edward W. Smykay, Donald J. Bowersox, and Frank H. Mossman, *Physical Distribution Management* (New York: The Macmillan Co., 1961), chap. iv.

[5]Two notable exceptions are: J. L. Heskett, "Costing and Coordinating External and Internal Logistics Activities," unpublished paper before joint seminar the Railway Systems and Management Association and the Transportation Research Forum, Chicago, October 6, 1964; and Frank H. Mossman and Newton Morton, *Logistics of Distribution Systems* (Boston: Allyn & Bacon, Inc., 1965), Part I.

distribution channels as being inherently endowed with duplication, waste, and inefficiency. The social justification for intermediaries has always appeared in doubt, leading to the general belief that one road to increasing marketing efficiency depended on elimination of middlemen. Despite this condemnation, specialized middlemen have survived and increased in importance.[6]

The intentions of this paper are limited to some observations concerning the problems of channel-wide physical distribution. One promising way to increase marketing efficiency is to improve physical movement between intermediaries. Advantages in operations result when physical flow is separated from other flows in the distribution process. Thus, a scheme for channel classification is presented. The functions necessary to complete physical exchange represent cost centers in the channel. Therefore, the second task is to examine exchange functions. Next, attention is focused upon the total channel distribution network. Finally, the objectives of the channel as a single system of action are examined.

CHANNEL CLASSIFICATION

Several classifications develop the idea of flow separation within the basic distribution channel. Two such classifications have been utilized to develop the framework presented here. The Vaile, Grether and Cox treatment directly engaged separation of eight flows which occur in the channel.[7] Breyer's recent grouping of channel members as trading and nontrading entities offers an approach to separation.[8]

The present approach singles out two flows. In order to accomplish satisfactory marketing, a flow of transaction-creating efforts and a flow of physical fulfillment efforts must exist. These two flows—physical fulfillment and transaction creating—are considered primary. All other flows in the distribution channel are considered secondary.

J. R. Commons differentiated elements of a bargaining transaction with the process of physical exchange.[9] The bargaining transaction was viewed as containing three steps: (1) negotiation—reaching a satisfactory agreement, (2) contract—establishment of obligations, and (3) administration—performance of obligations. Exchange, in contrast, was viewed as the mechanical and labor process of physical delivery.[10]

Separation of exchange fulfillment and transaction creation is based

[6] Reavis Cox, *Distribution in a High-Level Economy* (Englewood Cliffs, N.J.: Prentice-Hall, Inc., 1965), p. 51.

[7] Roland Vaile, E. T. Grether, and Reavis Cox, *Marketing in the American Economy* (New York: The Ronald Press Co., 1952), p. 113.

[8] Ralph F. Breyer, "Some Observations on Structural Formation and the Growth of Marketing Channels," in Reavis Cox, Wroe Alderson, Stanley J. Shapiro (eds.), *Theory in Marketing* (Homewood, Ill.: Richard D. Irwin, Inc., 1964), pp. 163–75.

[9] John R. Commons, *The Economics of Collective Action* (New York: The Macmillan Co., 1950) p. 53.

[10] *Ibid.*, p. 45.

upon the simple notion that a product may arrive physically but not arrive economically or legally. Factors increasing or decreasing the cost of physical flow have no respect for ownership boundaries. Conversely, advertising credit, personal selling and other transaction-creating efforts of marketing have little influence upon the economics of physical flow. The responsiveness of each primary flow to specialization are unique to the circumstances surrounding that flow. In any given marketing situation primary flows may best be accomplished by different middlemen. The most effective network for achieving profitable transactions may not be the most efficient arrangement of exchange intermediaries. Based upon specialization in primary flow, the distribution channel is classified as containing transaction channels and exchange channels.

The transaction channel consists of a grouping of intermediaries who engage in the establishment of trading. The goal of the transaction channel is to negotiate, contract, and administer trading on a continuing basis. Thus, the full force of creative marketing action exists within the transaction channel. Participants in transaction channel activities are marketing specialists.

The exchange channel contains a network of intermediaries engaged in the functions of physical movement. Participants in the exchange channel are physical distribution specialists. Their concern is one of solving problems of time and space at a total expenditure consistent to trading specifications.

This classification differs from Professor Breyer's to the extent his trading and nontrading channels may each engage in exchange. The difference in current classification and that of Vaile, Grether and Cox is one of emphasis between primary and secondary flows.

The tendency toward separation is easily observed in business practice. The best example is the factory branch office which carries no inventory. The office exists for the sole purpose of transaction creation. The physical exchange between seller and buyer may move in a variety of combinations of transport and storage depending upon value size of shipment, bulk, weight, perishability; plus time and location requirements. There is no economic justification for locating warehouses with each branch office. The network of branch offices is best selected to provide maximum transaction impact. The selection of exchange intermediaries is designed to achieve physical distribution economies. Examples of firms enjoying such separation benefits are Pillsbury, Heinz, Johnson & Johnson, and the E. F. MacDonald Company.

A second example of separation is found in retailing. It is now common for retailers to limit stocks to display models. Sales are negotiated based on a commitment to deliver at a particular time and place a specified model and color. While the transaction is initiated at a retail store, physical exchange may consist of direct shipment to the consumer's home from retailer's, distributor's, or factory warehouse. Such warehouses may be geographically located many miles from the point of transaction. Examples of this form of separation are J. L. Hudson, Macy's, and Polk Brothers.

A final example of separation comes from the rapidly growing mail-order industry. An order placed at a local catalog desk may be shipped from a distant factory direct to the buyer's home. While the flow pattern described is one of many observable arrangements in mail order, all such systems are designed to create separation and thereby specialization.

Separation of transaction and exchange increases the structural opportunities available for development of specialized channels. This does not mean separate legal enterprises are necessary to enjoy benefits of specialization. The degree of enterprise separation depends upon the necessity of specialization, economies of scale, available resources, and managerial capabilities. When a single enterprise engages both primary flows, specialization of management is required.

Transactions are never complete until physical exchange is fully administered. Depending upon the category of goods—convenience, shopping, or specialty—the exchange process may start in anticipation of, simultaneous with, or after actual negotiation is initiated. The final exchange act occurs in accord with specifications established during the negotiation phase of the transaction. Such exchange specifications relate to time, location or terms of transfer. Given any set of specifications, minimization of exchange expense is essential to achieve a mutually satisfactory transaction.

Contributions of efficient exchange are not limited to cost reduction. By achieving time and place utility, exchange can enhance transaction capabilities.[11] The ability to promise and provide dependable delivery of a proper assortment serves as a stimulant to agreement. Actual performance according to specifications creates a tendency toward continued transaction and the benefits of routinization. Thus, while present concern is with exchange mechanics, exchange capabilities may greatly enhance or dilute transaction potential.

CHANNEL FUNCTIONS OF EXCHANGE

Exchange goals are more readily stated than accomplished. Exchange exists to create an assortment of finished goods and to present such assortment at the proper location at the correct time.

Exchange flow in a channel is analogous to the workings of a ratchet wrench. Physical movement is designed for economies of one-way movement toward terminal user locations with scheduled stops occurring at a

---

[11]For two discussions of the impact of physical distribution on sales see: Wendell M. Stewart, "Physical Distribution: Key to Improved Volume and Profits," *Journal of Marketing,* January, 1965, pp. 67–68, and Thomas A. Staudt and Donald A. Taylor, *A Managerial Introduction to Marketing* (Englewood Cliffs, N.J.: Prentice-Hall, Inc., 1965), p. 222.

minimum of predetermined points. The frequency of such stops is determined, in part, upon specifications with respect to time, place, and assortment, and in part, upon alternate structures available for achieving desired results. Thus the exchange channel is subject to scrutiny by two measures: (1) Capability in time, place, and assortment closure; and (2) Evaluation of total cost expenditure between alternate structures capable of achieving closure. The fact exchange is concerned with physical properties makes quantification, experimentation, measurement, and evaluation more readily achieved than in the more complicated systems of transaction.

Several functions must be performed in the exchange process. Five such functions are singled out and discussed independent of performance point in a channel: (1) Adjustment; (2) Transfer; (3) Storage; (4) Handling; and (5) Communication.

The function of adjustment has received considerable treatment in marketing.[12] Adjustment is the aspect of exchange concerned with creating an assortment of finished goods. At some point in the exchange process goods must be concentrated, sorted, and dispersed to another level in the channel. Concentration refers to the collection of large lots of a single good or large groupings of several goods earmarked for final sale in an assortment. Sorting is the process of reducing large groupings into custom offerings. Dispersement consists of placing the custom assortments in the anticipated time and place perspective. The economies of specialization and the inherent risks of adjustment are two main justifications for the existence of middlemen.

The function of transfer constitutes the mechanics of collection and dispersement. A single good or an assortment of goods must be physically transported to achieve temporal and spatial value. The cost of transfer may be the greatest of all functions of exchange. Each transfer in the exchange process is a singularly conclusive act with associated costs. As such, the margin for error is narrow and the related penalties are great. It is not surprising to find specialized transfer intermediaries who engage in the mechanics of movement. Such specialists, in the form of motor, rail, water, and air carriers, engage in the specialization of movement accepting only performance risks. The risks of timing and directing the strategy of transfer remain with other intermediaries in the exchange channel.

Storage occurs because a great deal of concentration, sorting, and dispersement is in anticipation of future transaction. Given conditions of uncertainty in demand and supply, the exchange process must develop

---

[12]This concept has long standing in marketing literature. Two early treatments are found in: Percival White, *Scientific Marketing Management* (New York: Harper & Bros., 1927), and Fred E. Clark, *Readings in Marketing* (New York: The Macmillan Co., 1924). For refinement and expansion, see among others: Wroe Alderson, *Marketing Behavior and Executive Action* (Homewood, Ill.: Richard D. Irwin, Inc., 1957), chap. vii.

certain hedges in order to satisfy future transaction requirements. The risks in storage may be the greatest of all exchange functions since a certain depreciative factor occurs when inventories stand idle. A continuous exchange flow from processing through adjustment and on to consumption would be the least risky for all channel members. However, in a buyers' market continuous movement seldom exists. The exchange channel must be structured to postpone functions as long as possible without endangering transaction capabilities.

Handling may be the least risky of exchange functions. The expenses associated with handling are significant. Once a lot or an assortment of goods reaches a stopping point, shuffling begins. Cartons are moved in, placed, moved about, moved about some more, and hopefully finally moved out. The costs of handling are like the costs of transfer. Each handling has a separate and unique cost. Consequently, the fewer the total handlings, the lower the total cost. The economic justification for container and unitized loads stems from this basic fact.

Communication is a two-way function in the exchange process. In one direction messages relay the stimulus for exchange action. In the other direction communications monitor progress toward desired end results. From stimulant to feedback, the direct costs of communication are overshadowed by the implications of faulty message content. Since a great deal of exchange is initiated in anticipation, communication of overly optimistic potential may stimulate an exchange channel into a fever of ultimately useless work. Recent analysis of communications between channel members suggests such anticipation has a tendency to increase in amplification as it proceeds between consecutive intermediaries in an exchange network.[13]

In summary, successful exchange requires channel members to perform the functions of adjustment, transfer, storage, handling, and communication. Only through coordination of all functions are transaction specifications satisfied. Peter Drucker recently concluded that physical distribution contributes little if anything to the physical characteristics of a good product. It does, however, create the attributes of time and place—it brings the product to the customer.[14] Such attributes continue to be accomplished most efficiently through networks of intermediaries.

THE EXCHANGE NETWORK

Since a number of functions must be performed in the exchange process, each with related risks, it is not surprising that a number of individual enterprise units combine to create a channel or network. These enterprises are specialists in one or more exchange functions.

---

[13]See Jay W. Forrester, *Industrial Dynamics* (Cambridge, Mass.: The M.I.T. Press, 1961), p. 62.
[14]Peter Drucker, "The Economy's Dark Continent," *Fortune,* April, 1962, p. 103.

To various degrees each channel member enjoys rewards or suffers losses based upon the overall success of the channel. The intermediary serves in the capacity of specialist. His existence spreads the risk of a given endeavor.

Risk in an exchange network is not equally spread among all participants. A motor carrier performing one transfer function in a channel has relatively little risk with respect to ultimate transaction. A retailer has some risk related to the sale of a single product which he hedges by offering a wide asortment. In contrast, a processor or manufacturer of a few products may risk his survival on the capabilities of a movement channel.

This disproportionate spread of risk among channel members is of central importance in the exchange process. Some channel members have deeper vested interest in the ultimate accomplishment of successful exchange than other members. Therefore, they are forced to take more active interest and responsibility in channel destiny. Without guidance, a great many of the costs of exchange occur between channel members and legally outside the boundaries and traditional concerns of any single enterprise. Such costs must be controlled if the channel is to realize maximum exchange capabilities. However, control in an exchange channel is difficult to obtain since the only alternatives to ownership are persuasion or coercion.

Ownership, of course, consists of vertical integration of two or more consecutive links in the exchange channel by a single enterprise. The ultimate of vertical integration in an exchange channel would be a producer shipping via private transportation through his own storage points to factory sales outlets, who in turn handled the physical transfer to the consumer. The exact extent of vertical integration during the past two decades is difficult to appraise. There is increasing justification to conclude that perhaps the transaction channel has undergone more dramatic vertical integration than the movement channel. The most radical shift in types of intermediaries has been in the transfer channel between so-called agents and factory sales offices.[15] It likewise appears that merchant wholesalers have increased at the very time when vertical integration by large retailers and manufacturers was supposed to have eliminated their basis of economic justification.[16] The potential economies of vertical integration in exchange may not be offset by corresponding loss of innovative specialization and risk spreading.

The tactics of persuasion and coercion appear to offer the most practical methods for controlling exchange channel activities. Within the exchange channel, this basic need for common action under leadership guidance has been referred to as super-organization management.[17] While all firms have a desire to cooperate, individual profit orientation and legal bound-

---

[15]Cox, *op. cit.*, p. 55.

[16]*Ibid.*, p. 56.

[17]Heskett, *op. cit.*, p. 2.

aries seem to instill elements of conflict. In addition, there exists a degree of conflict over which member will assume financial responsibility for performing the more risky exchange functions. The analysis of motivation of conflict and cooperation in both trading and exchange channels is currently receiving substantial attention in the literature.[18] A review of such work is beyond the intentions of this paper. The essential point is that the ultimate survival of a channel may depend upon creative leadership.

A great deal of future improvement in marketing efficiency depends upon substantial increase in managerial concern with channel group objectives as opposed with preoccupation of the firm as an individual channel member.

OBJECTIVES OF EXCHANGE CHANNELS

As a competitive group, an exchange channel desires to complete the necessary functions of exchange in accord with some well-defined objectives. The objectives are singled out as: (1) minimum possible transfers; (2) maximum postponement in adjustment; and (3) minimum massed reserves.[19]

The objectives of minimum possible engagements encourage the least amount of transfer, handling, adjustment, and storage possible. While important to the total process, the costs of duplication in such functions rapidly accumulate. Thus, the fewer nodal points physical products flow through, the more inherently efficient the channel.

The objective of maximum postponement in adjustment encourages the holding of homogeneous concentrated lots as long as possible in the exchange process. Since a great deal of exchange activity is in anticipation of future transaction, the longer a concentration is maintained, the greater the ability to adjust custom assortments in various volumes. The ideal approach is to concentrate lots based upon transaction anticipation with postponement of sorting and dispersement until a firm commitment is at hand. The longer an exchange channel can postpone final adjustment, the more flexible the total exchange process. Remolding a previous established assortment adds ancillary costs to the total process.

The objective of minimum massed reserves may appear to stand in

---

[18]For example see: J. C. Palamountain, Jr., *The Politics of Distribution.* (Cambridge, Mass.: Harvard University Press, 1955); Valentine Ridgeway, "Administration of Manufacturer-Dealer Systems," *Administrative Science Quarterly*, March, 1957, pp. 464-83; Bruce Malle, "Conflict and Cooperation in Marketing Channels," in L. George Smith (ed.), *Reflections on Progress in Marketing, Proceedings American Marketing Association* (Chicago: American Marketing Association, 1964), pp. 65-85; and Bert C. McCammon, Jr., "Alternative Explanations of Institutional Change and Channel Evolution," in Stephen A. Greyser (ed.), *Toward Scientific Marketing, Proceedings American Marketing Association* (Chicago: American Marketing Association, 1963), pp. 477-90.

[19]A great deal of this section is based upon Alderson, *op. cit.*

contrast wth the objective of postponement. However, why hold homogeneous lots at consecutive levels in an exchange channel? For a long time it was fashionable to mass finished inventory at various levels of the channel in anticipation of transaction. In practice, there appears to have been extensive pressure on the part of trading groups for inventory support in each market as a prerequisite to successful transaction. The tendency is now toward the staging of a central supply as far geographically separated from the market as economically feasible. The rapid expansion of product offerings in all trade channels has created serious risks in holding reserves for each specialized market. Given conditions of erratic demand, the lowest total cost movement expenditure may well be expensive fast physical transport as late in the transaction process as technologically possible. Inventories in the total exchange channel must be minimized without diluting transaction support capabilities. Only if such minimization is achieved are the benefits of innovation encouraged and the forces of rigidity eliminated.

The objectives outlined above are channel-wide considerations. Their accomplishment embodies an understanding on the part of all enterprise members concerning the degree of interdependence necessary for efficient exchange. Lack of united effort to achieve these objectives leads to increased costs as members duplicate functions of exchange.

CONCLUSION

It has been suggested that issues of channel analysis are clarified by separation of transaction and exchange flows. While some enterprises engage in both transaction and exchange, the functions and objectives of exchange favor specialized intermediaries.

Within the legal and managerial boundaries of a given firm, significant advancements have been made in reducing the cost and improving the effectiveness of physical distribution. Many of these advancements have resulted from a willingness to discard outdated ideas concerning internal cost measurements and physical flow management. At best, these desirable adancements improve the short-range efficiency for individual firms. Development in exchange must expand to boundaries of the movement channel. Only when firms linked together for joint economic gain acknowledge the existence of duplicated and ancillary functions of exchange will the waste in movement be eliminated.

The exchange process is physical in nature representing something we know how to manipulate, mold, and perfect at today's level of knowledge. Perhaps the ultimate efficiency of exchange is more directly related to channel structure than trading as a result of superior quantification potential. Because so little attention has been devoted to exchange on a channel grouping basis, the prospects for improved marketing efficiency are encouraging.

In the case of highly branded or differentiated products, innovation for efficiency may result from manufacturers. Retailers, having substantial market acceptance, may initiate such action. Finally, in cases of wide assortments accumulated from small processers and distributed to small retailers, the wholesaler may provide the impetus for increasing exchange efficiency. The consumer cares very little about who receives the proceeds from a purchase. He does care about the total amount of such proceeds.

15. POSTPONEMENT, SPECULATION AND THE STRUCTURE OF DISTRIBUTION CHANNELS*

Louis P. Bucklin

THE CONCEPT OF SUBSTITUTABILITY

Underlying the logic of the principle to be developed is the hypothesis that economic interaction among basic marketing functions and between these functions and production provides much of the force that shapes the structure of the distribution channel. These interactions occur because of the capability of the various functions to be used as substitutes for each other within certain broad limitations. This capability is comparable to the opportunities available to the entrepreneur to use varying ratios of land, labor, and capital in the production of his firm's output. The substitutability of marketing functions may occur both within the firm and among the various institutions of the channel, for example, producers, middlemen, and consumers. This substitutability permits the work load of one function to be shrunk and shifted to another without affecting the output of the channel. These functional relationships may also be seen to be at the root of the "total cost" concept employed in the growing literature of the management of the physical distribution system [3, 9].

A familiar example of one type of substitution that may appear in the channel is the use of inventories to reduce the costs of production stemming from cyclical demand. Without the inventory, production could only occur during the time of consumption. Use of the inventory permits production to be spread over a longer period of time. If some institution of the channel senses that the costs of creating a seasonal inventory would be less than the savings accruing from a constant rate of production, it would seek to create such a stock and to retain the resulting profits. The consequence of this action is the formation of a new and alternate channel for the product.

The momentum of change, however, is not halted at this point. Unless

Journal of Marketing Research, February, 1965, pp. 26–31.

there is protection against the full brunt of competitive forces, the institutions remaining in the original, and now high-cost, channel will either be driven out of business or forced to convert to the new system as well. With continued competitive pressure the excess profits, initially earned by the institutions which innovated the new channel, will eventually be eliminated and total channel costs will fall.

In essence, the concept of substitutability states that under competitive conditions institutions of the channel will interchange the work load among functions, not to minimize the cost of some individual function, but the total costs of the channel. It provides, thereby, a basis for the study of distribution channels. By understanding the various types of interactions among the marketing functions and production that could occur, one may determine the type of distribution structure that should appear to minimize the total channel costs including those of the consumer. The principle of postponement-speculation, to be developed below, evaluates the conditions under which one type of substitution may occur.

POSTPONEMENT

In 1950, Wroe Alderson proposed a concept which uniquely related certain aspects of uncertainty and risk to time. He labeled this concept the "principle of postponement" and argued that it could be used to reduce various marketing costs [2]. Risk and uncertainty costs were tied to the differentiation of goods. Differentiation could occur in the product itself and/or the geographical dispersion of inventories. Alderson held that "the most general method which can be applied in promoting the efficiency of a marketing system is the postponement of differentiation . . . postpone changes in form and identity to the latest possible point in the marketing flow; postpone change in inventory location to the latest possible point in time." [1] Savings in costs related to uncertainty would be achieved "by moving the differentiation nearer to the time of purchase," where demand, presumably, would be more predictable. Savings in the physical movement of the goods could be achieved by sorting products in "large lots," and "in relatively undifferentiated states."

Despite its potential importance, the principle has received relatively little attention since it was first published. Reavis Cox and Charles Goodman [4] have made some use of the concept in their study of channels for house building materials. The Vaile, Grether, and Cox marketing text [10] also makes mention of it. As far as can be determined, this is the totality of its further development.

As a result, the principle still constitutes only a somewhat loose, and possibly misleading, guide to the study of the distribution channel structure. The major defect is a failure to specify the character of the limits which prevent it from being applied. The principle, which states that changes in form and inventory location are to be delayed to the latest possible moment, must also explain why in many channels these changes appear at the earliest. As it stands, the principle of postponement requires modification if it is to be applied effectively to the study of channels.

POSTPONEMENT AND THE SHIFTING OF RISK

If one views postponement from the point of view of the distribution channel as a whole, it may be seen as a device for individual institutions to shift the risk of owning goods to another. The manufacturer who postpones by refusing to produce except to order is shifting the risk forward to the buyer. The middleman postpones by either refusing to buy except from a seller who provides next day delivery (backward postponement), or by purchasing only when he has made a sale (forward postponement). The consumer postpones by buying from those retail facilities which permit him to take immediate possession directly from the store shelf. Further, where the consumer first contacts a number of stores before buying, the shopping process itself may be seen as a process of postponement—a process which advertising seeks to eliminate.

From this perspective it becomes obvious that every institution in the channel, including the consumer, cannot postpone to the latest possible moment. The channel, in its totality, cannot avoid ownership responsibilities. Some institution, or group of institutions, must continually bear this uncertainty from the time the goods start through production until they are consumed.

Since most manufacturers do produce for stock and the ownership of intermediate inventories by middlemen is characteristic of a large proportion of channels, it is clear that the principle of postponement can reach its limit very quickly. As a result, it provides no rationale for the forces which create these inventories. Hence, postponement is really only half a principle. It must have a converse, a converse equally significant to channel structure.

SPECULATION

This converse may be labeled the principle of speculation. It represents a shift of risk to the institution, rather than away from it. The principle of speculation holds that changes in form, and the movement of goods to forward inventories, should be made at the earliest possible time in the marketing flow in order to reduce the costs of the marketing system.

As in the case of postponement, application of the principle of speculation can lead to the reduction of various types of costs. By changing form at the earliest point, one makes possible the use of plants with large-scale economies. Speculation permits goods to be ordered in large quantities rather than in small frequent orders. This reduces the costs of sorting and transportation. Speculation limits the loss of consumer good-will due to stock-outs. Finally, it permits the reduction of uncertainty in a variety of ways.

This last point has already been well developed in the literature. It received early and effective treatment from Frank H. Knight [6]. He held that speculators, by shifting uncertainty to themselves, used the principle of grouping, as insurance, to transform it into the more manageable form of a relatively predictable risk. Further, through better knowledge of the risks to be handled and more informed opinion as to the course of future events, risk could be further reduced.

THE COMBINED PRINCIPLE

From the point of view of the distribution channel, the creation of inventories for holding goods before they are sold is the physical activity which shifts risk and uncertainty. Such inventories serve to move risk away from those institutions which supply, or are supplied by, the inventory. Such inventories, however, will not be created in the channel if the increased costs attending their operation outweigh potential savings in risk. Risk costs, according to the substitutability hypothesis, cannot be minimized if other costs increase beyond the savings in risk.

This discussion shows the principle of speculation to be the limit to the principle of postponement, and vice versa. Together they form a basis for determining whether speculative inventories, those that hold goods prior to their sale, will appear in distribution channels subject to competitive conditions. Operationally, postponement may be measured by the notion of delivery time. Delivery time is the number of days (or hours) elapsing between the placing of an order and the physical receipt of the goods by the buyer [9, p. 93]. For the seller, postponement increases, and costs decline, as delivery time lengthens. For the buyer, postponement increases, and costs decline as delivery time shortens. The combined principle of postponement-speculation may be stated as follows: A speculative inventory will appear at each point in a distribution channel whenever its costs are less than the net savings to both buyer and seller from postponement.

OPERATION OF THE PRINCIPLE

The following hypothetical example illustrates how the postponement-speculation principle can be applied to the study of distribution channels. The specific problem to be considered is whether an inventory, located between the manufacturer and the consumer, will appear in the channel. This inventory may be managed by the manufacturer, a consumer co-operative or an independent middleman.

Assume that trade for some commodity occurs between a set of manufacturers and a set of customers, both sets being large enough to insure active price competition. The manufacturers are located close to each other in a city some significant distance from the community in which the customers are situated. All of the customers buy in quantities sufficiently large to eliminate the possibility of savings from sorting. Manufacturing and consumption are not affected by seasonal variations. Assume, further, that production costs will not be affected by the presence of such an intermediate inventory.

To determine whether the intermediate inventory will appear, one must first ascertain the shape of the various relevant cost functions with respect to time. In any empirical evaluation of channel structure this is likely to be the most difficult part of the task. For present purposes, however, it will be sufficient to generalize about their character.

The costs incurred by the relevant functions are divided into two broad categories. The first includes those costs originating from activities associated with the potential inventory, such as handling, storage, interest, uncertainty, and costs of selling and buying if the inventory is operated by a middleman. It also includes those costs emanating from transportation, whether the transportation is direct from producer to consumer or routed through the inventory. All of these costs will, in turn, be affected by the particular location of the inventory between the producer and the consumer. In the present instance, it is assumed that the inventory will be located in the consumer city.

In general, this first category includes all the relevant costs incurred by the producer and intermediary, if any. These are aggregated in Figure 1. In this diagram, the ordinate represents the average cost for moving one unit of the commodity from the producer to the consumer. The abscissa measures the time in days for delivery of an order to the

FIGURE 1

AVERAGE COST OF DISTRIBUTING ONE UNIT OF
A COMMODITY TO A CUSTOMER WITH RESPECT
TO DELIVERY TIME IN DAYS

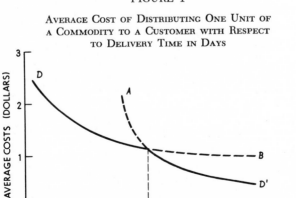

consumer after it has been placed. The curve *DB* measures the cost of using the speculative inventory to supply the consumer for the various possible delivery times. Curve *AD'* shows the cost of supplying the consumer direct without use of such an inventory. *DD'* is the minimum average cost achievable by either direct or indirect distribution of the commodity.

The diagram shows that *DD'* declines as the delivery time is allowed to increase [7]. With very short delivery times the intermediate inventory is absolutely necessary because only in this way can goods be rushed quickly to the consumer. Further, when virtually immediate delivery is required, the safety stock of the inventory must be kept high in order to prevent temporary stock-outs from delaying shipment. Also, delivery trucks must always be available for short notice. These factors create high costs.

As the delivery time to be allowed increases, it becomes possible to reduce the safety stocks, increase the turnover, and reduce the size of the facilities and interest cost. Further increases permit continued savings. Eventually, a point will be reached, *I* in Figure 1, where the delivery time will be sufficiently long to make it cheaper to ship goods directly from the factory to the consumer than to move them indirectly through the inventory. This creates the discontinuity at *I* as the costs maintaining the inventory and the handling of goods are eliminated.

In part, the steepness of the slope of *DD'* will be affected by the uncertainties of holding the inventory. Where prices fluctuate rapidly or goods are subject to obsolescence, these costs will be high. The extension of delivery time, in permitting the intermediate inventory to be reduced in size and eventually eliminated, should bring significant relief.

The second category of costs involves those emanating from the relevant marketing functions performed by the customers. Essentially, these

FIGURE 2

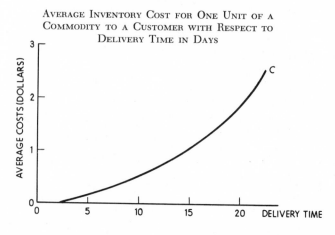

AVERAGE INVENTORY COST FOR ONE UNIT OF A COMMODITY TO A CUSTOMER WITH RESPECT TO DELIVERY TIME IN DAYS

costs will be those of bearing the risk and costs of operating any inventory on the customer's premises. These costs are shown as C on Figure 2, with the ordinate and abscissa labeled as in Figure 1.

The shape of C is one that increases with delivery time. The longer the delivery time allowed by the customer, the greater the safety shock he will have to carry. Such stock is necessary to protect against failures in transport and unpredictable surges in requirements. Hence, his costs will increase. The greater the uncertainty cost of inventory holding, the steeper will the slope of this function be.

Determination of the character of the distribution channel is made from the joint consideration of these two cost categories, C and DD'. Whether an intermediate inventory will appear in the channel depends upon the relationship of the costs for operating the two sets of functions and how their sum may be minimized. Functions $DD' + C$ on Figure 3 represent the sum of functions DD' and C. The diagram reveals, in this instance, that costs of postponement are minimized by use of a speculative inventory as the minimal cost point, M, falls to the left of I. If, however, the risk costs to the customer had been less, or the general cost of holding inventories at the customer's home (or plant site, as the case may be) had been lower, then C would be farther to the right. M would also shift to the right. With a sufficient reduction in consumer cost, M would appear to the right of the discontinuity, indicating that direct shipment in the channel would be the means to minimize postponement cost.

FIGURE 3

TOTAL OF AVERAGE DISTRIBUTING AND
CUSTOMER INVENTORY COSTS WITH RESPECT
TO DELIVERY TIME IN DAYS

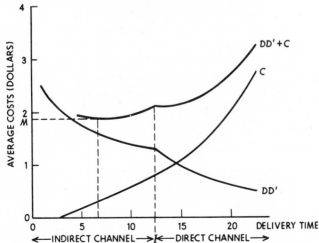

SIGNIFICANCE OF THE PRINCIPLE

As developed, the principle of postponement-speculation provides a basis for expecting inventories to be present in channels because of production and distribution time requirements. In particular, it treats the role of speculative inventories in the channel. The concept, as a consequence, extends beyond the physical flow of the goods themselves to the flow of their title. Speculative inventories create the opportunity for new institutions to hold title in the channel. Without such inventories, there may be little economic justification for a title-holding intermediary to enter the channel. The economic need to have such an inventory in the physical flow opens the door to a middleman to show whether he is capable of reducing the risk cost of that inventory below the level attainable by either the producer or some consumer cooperative.

The presence of an inventory in the channel for either collecting, sorting, or dispersing does not create the same type of opportunity for a title-making intermediary to appear in the channel. Such inventories are not speculative in character. They do not need to hold uncommitted stocks of goods available for general sale in order to fulfill their purpose. For example, the REA Express, the parcel post system, freight forwarders, and even the Greyhound Bus Corporation's freight system sort a substantial volume of goods through many nonspeculative type inventories each day. Milk producers establish handling depots where bottled milk is transferred from large, long-distance vehicles to city delivery trucks. Catalog sellers discharge full truck shipments upon the post offices of distant cities where customers reside. None of these inventories involves the risk of unsold goods. None of these inventories provides the basis for the emergence of a title-holding middleman.

From this perspective, the principle of postponement-speculation may be regarded as a concept which broadens the channel analyst's understanding of the intimate relationship between title and physical flows. The intertwining of the roles of ownership and the holding of speculative stocks provides a fundamental rationale for the position of the merchant middleman. The principle of postponement-speculation, as a consequence, can be employed to provide at least part of the explanation for the number of ownership stages in the channel. This, of course, is one of the basic questions toward which traditional distribution analysis is directed [5].

In this light, for example, the principle may be of use in explaining the emergence of an "orthodox channel of distribution." This concept, developed by Shaw [8], was used to characterize the nature of the distribution channel through which a large proportion of products traveled, to wit: the manufacturer-wholesaler-retailer route. That such a concept should emerge to characterize products, whose sorting needs are different because of diverse physical characteristics and market reach, is of extreme interest. Similarities among channels for different products implies that forces, which may not vary significantly among many types of goods, should be sought as explanatory variables of channel structure. Since many groups of consumer goods generate similar temporal types of risk, the principle of postponement-speculation may provide a major explanation for this phenomenon.

TESTING THE PRINCIPLE

The principle of postponement-speculation will not be easy to test for a number of reasons. First of all, it is normative. It is derived from assumptions of profit maximization and predictions are based upon what firms should do. Second, it approximates the real world only when the channel environment is sufficiently competitive to produce a variety of price-product-delivery time offers. Finally, it cannot predict the necessary time delays that occur in the channel for new facilities to be built or old ones abandoned.

Despite these problems, a number of hypotheses may be generated from the model and subjected to evaluation by surveys of existing channels. These surveys would locate any intermediate, speculative inventory in the channel and measure the time elapsing between the placing of an order by, and its delivery to, the customer. Use of industrial or commodity channels would undoubtedly be the best initial subjects for the surveys. The confounding effects of collecting, sorting, and dispersing in consumer channels will make the impact of the principle of postponement-speculation more difficult to isolate.

Six hypotheses which could be tested in this manner follow:

1. The shorter the delivery time, the greater the probability the channel will include an intermediate, speculative inventory.
2. The shorter the delivery time, the closer any speculative stock will be to the consumer.
3. The shorter the distance between a customer and a speculative stock, the greater the probability of a second such inventory in the channel.
4. Products which are heavy, bulky and inexpensive are likely to flow through channels with more intermediate, speculative inventories than products with the opposite characteristics.
5. Products which consumers find expensive to store on their premises, but whose use is both urgent and difficult to forecast, have a greater probability of passing through an intermediate, speculative inventory than products with the opposite characteristics.
6. The greater the inelasticity of consumer and/or producer cost with respect to changes in delivery time, the greater the stability of the most efficient channel type over time.

All of these hypotheses are subject to the *ceteris paribus* limitation.

Tests, as a result, should include only those channels operating under reasonably similar economic conditions. This is particularly important with respect to the distance between the producer and the consumer. Variations in this factor will affect the cost of providing any given delivery time. Channels which traverse longer distances, in other words, are likely to require more speculative inventories than those which move goods less extensively.

The *ceteris paribus* limitation also contains an important implication beyond that of the problems of testing. Consideration of this limitation provides the rationale for the presence of several different types of channels supplying the same type of product to a given group of customers. Producers, for example, provisioning some market from a distance, may be forced to use channels distinct from their competitors located adjacent to the customers. This diversity of channels may also be produced by imperfections in competition as well as variations in the urgency of demand among consumers in the market. Those who can easily tolerate delays in delivery are likely to use a different channel from those patronized by customers with dissimilar personalities or capabilities.

IMPLICATIONS OF THE PRINCIPLE

The principle of postponement-speculation, in addition to providing a basis for developing hypotheses for empirical testing, makes it possible to do some *a priori* generalizing concerning the type of channel structure changes one may expect to see in the future. Any force, or set of forces, which affects the types of costs discussed may be sufficient to move the balance from speculation to postponement, or vice versa.

One type of change, already occurring and which may be expected to spread in the future, rests upon the relationship between the cost of transportation and speed. Rapidly evolving methods of using air transport economically and efficiently are serving to narrow the spread between the cost of high-speed transportation and low-speed transportation. This has the effect of reducing the relative advantage of speculation over postponement. Hence, intermediate inventories will tend to disappear and be replaced by distribution channels which have a direct flow.

The increasing proliferation of brands, styles, colors, and price lines is another type of force which will affect the balance. This proliferation increases the risk of inventory holding throughout the entire channel, but particularly at those points closest to the consumer. Retailers will attempt to minimize this risk by reducing the safety stock level of their inventories and relying more upon speedy delivery from their suppliers. The role of the merchant wholesaler, or the chain-store warehouse, will become increasingly important in this channel. Indeed, there will probably be increasing efforts on the part of retailers to carry only sample stocks in those items where it is not absolutely necessary for customers to take immediate delivery. General Electric, for example, is experimenting with wholesaler-to-consumer delivery of large appliances. Drugstores, where the role of the pharmacist appears to be slowly changing from one of compounding prescriptions to inventorying branded specialties, will become further dependent upon ultra-fast delivery from wholesalers.

Those stores, such as discount houses, which are successfully able to resist the pressure toward carrying wide assortments of competing brands are likely to utilize channels of distribution which differ significantly from their full-line competitors. Large bulk purchases from single manufacturers can be economically delivered directly to the discount house's retail facilities. Where warehouses are used in discount house channels they can serve stores spread out over a far greater geographical area than would be normally served by a wholesaler. Such stores are also apt to find their market segments not only in middle income range families, but also among those consumers who tend to be heavily presold by manufacturer advertising, or who simply are less finicky about the specific type of item they buy.

A final possible trend may spring from consumers who find that their own shopping costs represent too great an expenditure of effort with respect to the value received from postponement. As a result, such consumers are likely to turn more and more to catalog and telephone shopping. Improved quality control procedures by manufacturers and better means of description in catalogs could hasten this movement. The acceptance of Sears telephone order services in large cities testifies that many individuals are prone to feel this way. If the movement were to become significantly enlarged, it could have a drastic effect upon the existing structure of distribution.

SUMMARY

The study of distribution channels and why they take various forms is one of the most neglected areas of marketing today. Part of the neglect may be due to the absence of effective tools for analysis. The principle of postponement-speculation is offered in the hope that it may prove useful in this regard and stimulate work in the area.

The principle directly treats the role of time in distribution and, indirectly, the role of distance as it affects time. The starting point for the development of the constructs of the principle may be found in the work of Alderson and Knight [1, 2, 6]. Postponement is measured by the change of delivery time in the shipping of a product. Increasing the delivery time decreases postponement costs for the seller, increases them for the buyer, and vice versa. Justification and support for the relationships suggested between the costs of marketing functions and delivery time may be found in the recent literature of physical distribution.

The principle reveals the effect upon channel structure of the interaction between the risk of owning a product and the physical functions employed to move the product through time. It holds that, in a competitive environment, the costs of these functions be minimized over the entire channel, not by individual function. The minimum cost and type of channel are determined by balancing the costs of alternative delivery times against the cost of using an intermediate, speculative inventory. The appearance of such an inventory in the channel occurs whenever its additional costs are more than offset by net savings in postponement to the buyer and seller.

REFERENCES

1. Wroe Alderson, *Marketing Behavior and Executive Action,* Homewood, Ill.: Richard D. Irwin, Inc., 1957, p. 424.
2. ———, "Marketing Efficiency and the Principle of Postponement," *Cost and Profit Outlook,* Vol. 3 (September, 1950).
3. Stanley H. Brewer and James Rosenweig, "Rhochematics," *California Management Review,* Vol. 3 (Spring, 1961), pp. 52–71.
4. Reavis Cox and Charles S. Goodman, "Marketing of Housebuilding Materials," *The Journal of Marketing,* Vol. 21 (July, 1956), pp. 55–56.
5. William R. Davidson, "Channels of Distribution—One Aspect of Marketing Strategy," *Business Horizons,* Special Issue—First International Seminar on Marketing Management, February, 1961, pp. 85–86.
6. Frank H. Knight, *Risk, Uncertainty and Profit.* Boston: Houghton Mifflin Co., 1921, pp. 238–39, 255–58.
7. John F. Magee, "The Logistics of Distribution," *Harvard Business Review,* Vol. 38 (July–August, 1960), pp. 97–99.
8. Arch W. Shaw, "Some Problems in Market Distribution," *The Quarterly Journal of Economics,* August, 1912, pp. 727.
9. See Edward W. Smykay, Donald J. Bowersox, and Frank J. Mossman, *Physical Distribution Management.* New York: Macmillan Co., 1961, ch. iv.
10. Roland S. Vaile, Ewald T. Grether, and Reavis Cox, *Marketing in the American Economy.* New York: Ronald Press Co., 1952, pp. 149–50.

Suggested additional AMA readings

Baligh, Helmy H. "A Theoretical Framework for Channel Choice," in *Marketing and Economic Development.* Chicago: American Marketing Association, September, 1965.

Bucklin, Louis P. "Postponement, Speculation and the Structure of Distribution Channels," *Journal of Marketing Research,* February, 1965, pp. 26–31.

———, and Halpert, Leslie. "Exploring Channels of Distribution for Cement with the Principle of Postponement-Speculation," in *Marketing and Economic Development.* Chicago: American Marketing Association, 1965.

Christian, Richard C. "Three-Step Method to Better Distribution Channel Analysis," *Journal of Marketing,* October, 1958, pp. 191–92.

LaLonde, Bernard J. "'The Logistics of Retail Location," *The Social Responsibilities of Marketing*, pp. 567–75. Chicago: American Marketing Association, 1961.

McCammon, Bert C., Jr. "The Emergence and Growth of Contractually Integrated Channels in the American Economy," in *Marketing and Economic Development*. Chicago: American Marketing Association, 1965.

McVey, Phillip. "Are Channels of Distribution What the Textbooks Say?" *Journal of Marketing*, January, 1960, pp. 61–65.

Stern, Louis W. "Channel Control and Inter-Organization Management," in *Marketing and Economic Development*. Chicago: American Marketing Association, 1965.

Part IV

MANAGEMENT OF BUSINESS LOGISTICS

Within the broad framework of business logistics, the principal ingredients are the management of transportation and inventories. Other activities such as forecasting, order processing, and material handling are supporting activities to this movement and storage and act to reduce total logistics cost and improve customer service. The process of improving distribution costs has led to the analysis of all systemic factors affecting the economics of delivering goods to the customer in the most effective manner.

In a broad discussion of physical distribution management, Berg (16) in "Designing the Distribution System" examines decisions from an internal, external, and environment viewpoint. Lewis (17) in "A Business Logistics Information and Accounting System for Marketing Analysis" suggests a data system which will facilitate the analysis of the distribution-related activities in marketing. Bowersox (18) discusses "The Role of the Marketing Executive in Physical Distribution." Finally, Cascino (19) in "Top Management Looks at Physical Distribution" discusses the corporate organization for physical distribution from the point of view of the top marketing administrator. He recommends awareness of the total order-delivery cycle.

16. DESIGNING THE DISTRIBUTION SYSTEM*

Thomas L. Berg

INTRODUCTION

Marketing management suffers from schizophrenia. Students of the firm are encouraging corporate psychoses identified by the classic syndrome:

*From *The Social Responsibilities of Marketing*, American Marketing Association, December, 1961.

(1) loss of contact with company environments and (2) disintegration of the whole properties of corporate organisms. The disease is amenable to treatment. This study is intended as a partial prescription, although it is not to be construed as any sort of a panacea.

To see the nature and origin of the malady in more concrete terms, it is necessary to understand how the total company is linked to its environment.

THE FIRM AS AN OPERATING SYSTEM

Any manufacturing enterprise can be viewed as an input-output system consisting of three parts: (1) the *internal organization* of the firm, (2) the company *environment,* and (3) various kinds of *external organizations* serving to link the internal organization with its economic milieu for the interorganizational transmission and processing of inputs and outputs.

Connections with suppliers, networks of financial intermediaries, and trade channels are examples of external organizations. Although they may not appear on company charts or in manuals, these should be regarded as logical extensions to the internal organization of the firm. Internal and external organizations are similar in that both deal with economic functions performed by interdependent human agents requiring motivation and coordination through communication. Both involve continuous personal relationships, routinized tasks, and stable expectations of reciprocal performance.

Failure to pay due respect to the systematic nature of the enterprise and to the fundamental similarities between internal and external organizations has resulted in schizoid thinking in management and marketing. Management theorists have been preoccupied with problems of *internal organization* and have failed to show how the firm is connected to its environment via externally organized linkages. An unnatural cleavage between internal and external aspects of structure has developed in the management literature.

Administrative and organizational theories seem to have concentrated upon the administration of single organizations and have not specifically recognized that a system of separate organizations requires administration also. It is suggested . . . that that body of theory and research which contributes to an understanding of the administrative process in single organizations is pertinent to the administration of primary and secondary organizations.[1]

Over the years, a handful of people have come to suggest that the full development of organization theory awaits the day when management theorists explicitly bring environmental entities and external organizations into their analyses. The sire of this thought appears to be Chester Barnard.

---

[1]Valentine F. Ridgway, "Administration of Manufacturer-Dealer Systems," *Administrative Science Quarterly,* Vol. 1 (March, 1957), pp. 466–67.

The conception of organization at which I arrived in writing *The Functions of the Executive* was that of an integrated aggregate of actions and interactions having a continuity in time. Thus I rejected the concept of organization as comprising a rather definite group of people whose behavior is coordinated with reference to some explicit goal or goals. On the contrary, I included in organization the actions of investors, suppliers, and customers or clients. Thus the material of organization is personal services, i.e., actions contributing to its purposes.[2]

Barnard's words have apparently fallen on deaf ears. Administrative theorists are concentrating more on refining theories of internal organization and less on extending and testing their notions in external realms. But the student of marketing is equally responsible for the observable symptoms of schizophrenia.

In contrast to the management theorists' focus on internal aspects of business systems, marketers have been preoccupied with environmental forces and external trading channels without clarifying how these tie in to problems of internal administration and organization. Marketing academicians seem to appreciate the need of some model for building and operating trade channels, but few have recognized the potential role of organization theory in its design. Businessmen in marketing seem to know intuitively that channel building is an organizational problem, although few acknowledge the need for a model to guide them in their organizing.

As a result, trends in management and marketing thinking become more and more divergent. To bring about some convergence and to assure that both disciplines reverse the trend to schizophrenia, it is necessary to (*a*) persuade the internally oriented administrative theorists to consider the application of their ideas to external-environmental entities and (*b*) convince marketers to draw more heavily on internally oriented theories for insights into building and operating external marketing systems. This study takes the distributive subsystem of the firm as an example of the applicability of organization theory to external systems.

THE DISTRIBUTION SUBSYSTEM

The term "trade channel" is often reserved to the network of external entities in a company's distribution setup. In this study, the term "distribution system" embraces all elements of the internal-external-environmental triad. Corporate marketing staffs and field sales forces are elements of internal organization; segments of ultimate consumer markets are the key environmental sectors; and retail merchants and other trade intermediaries make up the external organization. This study attempts to show that useful models of distribution systems can be designed with the help of organization theory.

[2]Chester I. Barnard, *Organization and Management* (Cambridge, Mass.: Harvard University Press, 1948), pp. 112–13.

Today, distribution systems are developed more by intuition than design. In part, this accounts for widespread cases of ineffective performance of trade management functions. Actual channel formation, budgeting for distribution, the setting of distributor's margins, the appraisal of dealer performance and similar management tasks could be performed more effectively if marketing managers had distributive models to guide them in the day-to-day administration of trading functions and trading relationships.

For many reasons, the basic idea that distribution models might be designed by drawing upon organization theory has not been widely recognized nor warmly embraced. The notion is still a relatively new one accepted by a fairly small group of people. Those who have heard of the idea often seem not to have grasped its full significance. The understanding of some has been barred by the persistence of traditional perspectives on trade channels. Those congenial to the basic idea may not know how to push it to the level of operational reality. Lack of know-how simply prevents others from seeing that the approach is feasible. Those that agree to its feasibility may be reluctant to devote the time, energy, and cash to what inevitably is a difficult design job. Some apparently see the feasibility of the notion but do not regard the approach as useful on pragmatic grounds. Still others may object on philosophical bases, for when organization theory is pushed far enough into market relationships difficult questions concerning prevailing concepts of competition are bound to arise.

The purpose of this study is simply to overcome a few of these barriers to acceptance of the fundamental proposition. The chief test applied in the study is the test of feasibility. As a purely technical matter, organization theory *can* be meaningfully applied to external distribution systems, and not only to direct manufacturer-dealer organizations. In the process of demonstrating feasibility, insights into the more intractable pragmatic and philosophical issues are also revealed.

NATURE OF THE STUDY

This study focuses on the contactual, or trading, aspects of distribution as opposed to the logistics, or physical distribution, dimensions of the problem. It is nonsituational, i.e., the study is not restricted in scope to a particular product, institution, or historical period. It is addressed to marketers in manufacturing firms, although the ideas may also be of interest to others.

Few businessmen can yet verbalize their opinions and attitudes toward the application of organization theory to the design of distributive models. Therefore, personal interviews could not be used as a sole method of research. Information had to be gleaned piecemeal from a variety of sources—including protracted informal interviews with some

150 marketing executives and teachers, widely scattered secondary sources, and pure cogitation.

In effect, the study attempts to present elements of prudent practice within the unifying framework of organization theory. It does not describe any approach taken by a known manufacturer.

ELEMENTS IN THE DESIGN PROCESS

The process of designing a distributive model for a producer is envisaged as unfolding in five interrelated stages: (1) factoring the company-wide strategic situation, (2) converting key factors into functional prerequisites for the system, (3) grouping individual tasks into work units, (4) allocating tasks to appropriate functionaries, and (5) designing a structure of relationships to provide loci of distributive authority and responsibility within the work structure erected in the previous stages.

In the study, separate chapters are devoted to each of these elements and an integrating case is used to help synthesize the materials as the process unfolds.

Step one—Factoring the strategic situation. Early in the research, comparative studies of existing systems were undertaken with the aim of accounting for the sometimes marked interfirm differences in distribution practices observable in many industries. Those variables were then abstracted which seemed to serve as decision-making constraints for a wide variety of the firms studied. These fell into two broad classes: (*a*) the nature and interests of various enrivonmental entities as interpreted by top management, and (*b*) factors relating to the company's resource base. Environmental entities and company resources are related through broad marketing strategy to the functional necessities and structural features of distribution systems. Environmental entities include stockholders, employees and their unions, supplier interests, trade associations, governments, competitors, and ultimate consumers. The resource base refers especially to finances and manpower but also includes material, spatial, temporal, and other resources. In the study, these factors are arranged and presented in meaningful sequence, and illustrations are provided to suggest the possible impact of each variable on channel function or structure. The goal was to help the manager conduct a comprehensive position audit for his own particular firm in its unique competitive market setting in order to isolate key bits of information which might provide clues as to appropriate distributive structure in the specific case. The study thus offers a method of attack for factoring a firm's strategic situation as well as illustrating the potentialities for interfirm differences in distribution systems.

Step two—Converting key factors into activity requirements. The research revealed that surprisingly few producers can meaningfully reply to the question, "What do you want your distribution setup to do for you?" It may be suggested here that until managers can verbalize the nature of the *work* they want performed by distribution systems, there can be little hope for real application of organization theory to trading networks.

Yet, the study offers guides for developing the inferential value of key factors uncovered in step one in sufficient detail to permit the generation of a fairly clear-cut list of activities to be performed by the yet-to-be-designed distribution system. At this point in the study, the integrating case is also introduced to illustrate how one firm actually posited its channel tasks in a simplified situation.

Step three—Grouping tasks into work units. This step involves a straightforward adaptation of organization theory, which alternatively depicts the process as one of a *division of labor* or of *grouping* tasks together in a meaningful fashion. No real problems of applying organization theory were encountered. However, there is clear evidence that the channel analyst might profit from taking this step very seriously. Traditional channel discourses, for example, have tended to stress specialization solely on the basis of function. Organization theory demands adequate attention to alternative modes of specialization, i.e., by product, by customer, by time, by location, by process, and by composite patterns of these basic varieties. All of the alternatives are relevant to distribution systems as well as to internal organization. Furthermore, channel planners perhaps stress short-term efficiency considerations too much in deciding what kind of task-split might be effected with the trade. Organizational theorists call attention to the needs for structural coordination, for promoting cooperation and reducing conflict, for recognizing the vagaries of local conditions, and other criteria for picking proper kinds and degrees of work specialization.

There is reason to assume that managers would uncover a much wider range of distribution alternatives and would probably end up by delegating more of the overall distributive job to tradesmen if they self-consciously applied the broader perspectives of organization theory to this step in the design of distribution systems. Finally, some varieties of organization theory focus first on the work and secondly on the worker. Classical institutional and commodity approaches to trade channels seem to have reversed the order of analysis.

Step four—Allocating tasks to middlemen. In matching work and worker, the best procedural approach seems to be to begin with segmenting the end markets to be served and then to progress upward through a process of sequential segmentation in intermediate markets until the intervening work structure can be made to tie together with the producer's internal organization.

At each stage of this process of closing gaps separating the producer from his ultimate markets, a set of interrelated issues must be resolved.

All alternative middlemen must first be *recognized* as alternatives. This is less obvious and more difficult than it appears. Semantic traps, statistical fictions, informational gaps, trained incapacities, managerial impatience and other barriers to creativity befog and bury alternatives from view. Brainstorming and other alternative-producing techniques, of course, are relevant in overcoming this problem.

With the alternatives before him, the manager must sort out ineligible types of outlets, drawing upon earlier key factors, activity requirements, and preliminary grouping analysis for screening criteria. Next, the remaining eligible outlet types can often be arrayed meaningfully in order of their apparent suitability to the producer, using the same criteria.

At this juncture, several additional types of questions often need to be answered before proceeding to another stage of the vertical channel stretch, e.g., whether there are economies of scale for each outlet type, how many of each type will be required, and what areal coverage pattern should be used. Since many of the variables used to resolve the latter issues lend themselves to quantification, some companies have been able to program them for computer solutions.

This set of decisions, made at successive stages in bridging the vertical gap between customers and the producer, completes the steps involved in planning the structure of distributive *work*. Before going further, however, the study discusses principles and procedures which serve as possible checks on the adequacy of the activity structure erected thus far on paper. The final step is to define desired relationships between individuals and institutions in the distribution system to provide loci of authority and responsibility as a basis for cooperative action.

Step five—Designating appropriate structural relationships. As a starting point in performing this step, the producer must know specifically what kinds of activities need to be controlled in order to comply with law, to ensure adequate profits, to generate goodwill and repeat business for his brands, to keep risk within limits, and to provide for effective coordination of his overall marketing program. Next, the producer must identify the sources of his capacity for influencing power patterns in the distribution system. These sources are rooted in governmental sanctions, specific laws, the strength of the consumer franchise held by the producer, and similar factors.

Basically, he now faces two alternatives for structural action. He can either try to accumulate market power which will then be exercised unilaterally to exact the compliance of middlemen, or he can undertake to create conditions under which authority may safely be dispensed in the system. In short, the alternatives are either to reserve authority from tradesmen or to delegate distributive authority to them. There are an infinite number of possible ways to mix these two basic alternatives. In this study, the outright ownership of facilities, existence of concubine outlets, preretailing practices, widespread consumer deals, and fair-trade arrangements are viewed as manifestations of the "reservation of authority" phenomenon. The delegation alternatives involve outright contractual or other specification of intended delegations, and these steps may be supplemented by the provision of facilitating and auxiliary service units (e.g., distributor training groups and dealer advisory councils) which help all parties to hold the exercise of authority within responsible bounds. The specific pattern of reservation-delegation devices chosen by the producer will depend on the way in which power has come to be institutionalized in the particular work structure he has put together, on the relative size and bargaining strength of producer and middlemen, on the past history of cooperation and conflict with similar patterns of tradesmen, and related factors.

When the five steps of the model-building process have been completed, the overall structure can then be described in charts and manuals. Job descriptions and man specifications for middlemen may also prove useful as guides to implementation of the model.

CONCLUSION

In very skeletal fashion, these five steps to the organizational design of distribution systems represent the ground covered in this study. Chester Barnard's basic idea is shown to be operationally meaningful; as a technical proposition, organization theory can usefully be extended to the design of external systems. But the task is just as difficult, frustrating, and time-consuming as it is in internal analyses—perhaps more so.

Yet the approach is practical for most firms. Organization theory provides a systematic and rational basis for superseding many of today's intuitive approaches to channel building. It is a body of doctrine that respects the inherent uniqueness of companies while providing guidelines for both orthodox and unconventional distribution systems. And it allows us to deal with both the *work* to be done in the system and the human *relationships* important to that performance.

Step-by-step application of concepts from organizational theory helps in the discovery of gaps in traditional ways of thinking about distribution. At the same time, it aids in uncovering more distributive alternatives and in providing criteria for choosing between them, it encourages the challenging of old concepts which may have outlined their usefulness, and it leads to a fuller understanding of the implications of past, present, and future trading actions.

There are many additional ways in which administrative theory can be effectively used to improve the management of distribution systems. Knowledge of institutional leadership and control in internal realms needs to be further extended, and perhaps modified, to apply in all external systems. By breaking down the walls tending to separate marketing from the field of general administration, marketers can also find themselves testing and improving administrative theory. The problem of choosing from alternative theories of organization still exists today. Perhaps further attempts to apply these theories to external systems could contribute to the unification of divergent threads.

This study was one test of organization theory in an external setting. The conclusion is that organization theory stands up better under analysis than does the marketer's concepts of distribution.

Increased awareness of the general applicability of administrative and organization theory to external systems may encourage further inter-disciplinary contributions to marketing and management. Industrial relations specialists could collaborate with marketers, for instance, in exploring points of similarity and difference between employee-union relationships within the firm and the extra-firm relationships between merchants and their trade associations. Something akin to collective bargaining is said to take place in some trades with respect to the setting of distributor margins and other issues. It would be interesting to pursue this further. Sociologists are now attempting to apply insights from general studies of bureaucracy to manufacturer-dealer relations. The concept of reference group behavior could perhaps be investigated more thoroughly for its relevance to trade channels. The anthropologist's idea of tangent relations and tangent institutions might provide further insights into the design and operation of distribution systems.

In short, recognition of the fact that organization theory offers immediate and practical help to manufacturers in the design of all distribution systems should open many doors for further research and remedy present tendencies toward schizophrenia in understanding business needs and company practices.

17. A BUSINESS LOGISTICS INFORMATION AND ACCOUNTING SYSTEM FOR MARKETING ANALYSIS*

Richard J. Lewis

BACKGROUND OF THE RESEARCH

Historically cost analysts have attempted to quantify distribution costs by reclassifying the accountant's natural accounts into marketing function cost accounts. Once derived, the functional accounts are assigned by standard unit costs to the various products, customers, and order

*From *Marketing and Economic Development* (Chicago: American Marketing Association, September, 1965), pp. 722–26.

sizes. The primary limitations of current methodology stem from the following:

1. Since the standard unit costs are often derived from historical costs of a single or multiple periods, management must choose a period which is "typical." That is, the costs in the period cannot be extremely high or low but must represent a "normal" cost of performing an activity.
2. The construction of standard costs as averages may cause the standard unit to represent wide ranges of cost variations which are hidden.
3. The third limitation arises from the tendency of cost analysts to ignore geographic cost variations while concentrating on variations among products, customer types, and order sizes.
4. Lastly it is important to note that the breakdown of natural accounts into functional accounts and their subsequent assignment by standard cost units to customers, products, etc., is not a continuous process and is made *after* the data have been accumulated. Herein lies the source of major limitations to distribution cost analysis. Where production cost analysis starts with multiple cost centers representing the source of costs and works toward aggregate costs, distribution cost analysis starts with the aggregate and works backwards toward the source. As previously mentioned, this reallocation of aggregate costs results in a loss of accuracy in determining distribution costs variations at their source.

THE PROPOSED INFORMATION SYSTEM

The information system developed in this research is an attempt to overcome many of the limitations present in current methods of distribution cost analysis. The primary objective of the information system is to provide geographic cost and revenue centers for the collection of marketing data which are small enough to reflect cost and revenue variations and yet are large enough to be feasible.

CONSTRUCTION OF THE INFORMATION CENTERS

The geographic information centers were developed from the one degree latitude and longitude lines which cross the United States. These lines form a system of 1° latitude and longitude quadrilaterals which cover the United States. Each 1° quadrilateral was subdivided into 256 subblocks. The number of subblocks is the result of dividing each degree latitude and longitude into 16 parts. The size of the final control units varies from 4.3 miles by 2.9 miles between the 49th and 48th degree parallels to 4.3 by 3.9 miles between the 25th and 24th parallels. Although the statute-mile size of the spherical control units varies in size from north to south, they are a constant size of 3.75′ of latitude and longitude. After subdividing the degrees of latitude and longitude the resulting rows and columns of subblocks were numbered by a vertical and horizontal scale with the origin at the northwest corner of the United States. This results in a spherical grid system of approximately 243,700 unique block locations covering the United States. Since all of the control units were originally derived from latitude and longitude measurements, the coding system of block numbers not only gives a unique location number but also provides a modified Cartesian coordinate system for measurement of relative location and distance between centers of blocks.

APPLICATIONS

APPLYING THE CONTROL UNITS TO CORPORATE RECORDS

The application of the control units to marketing analysis was performed by taking the sales orders and freight documents of a national manufacturer of industrial products for one year and reclassifying them as if the company had been using the spherical grid information system. This requires the identification of the grid block location number for each customer, distribution point and manufacturing point of the company, and the reporting of all grid block points of origin and destination on all the documents. The spherical grid block code requires six digits—three to identify a block's vertical position and three to identify its horizontal position. By adding two more digits, an eight-digit customer code is developed which not only identifies each customer but also locates him and provides a relative measure of the distance involved in serving him either by direct factory shipment or from alternate distribution points.

Since the sales order, freight bills, and other internal documents show the product's quantity, price, customer, carrier and shipment charges, and date of transactions, the use of the grid block code on internal company records automatically provides this information for each geographic control unit. Therefore, certain costs of serving specific markets (control units) are not hidden in averages but are available for analysis and potential control. Thus the use of standardized geographic coding of marketing records results in a geographically integrated marketing information system of internal records and, hence, makes it possible to merge the records of various marketing activities.

SOME APPLICATIONS OF THE SPHERICAL GRID SYSTEM
DETERMINING GEOGRAPHICALLY VARIABLE COSTS

Let me now turn to some specific findings of the research using the spherical control units. The first application of the system was its use in identifying those physical distribution costs which are geographically variable. In this application, two of the company's products were selected and their distribution costs to 99 control units were determined for shipments which had occurred from the factory to a distribution point and then to the customers. The physical distribution costs studied included transportation costs, storage costs, handling costs, packing list costs, order processing costs and a 6 percent pipeline interest cost on goods while in the process of being shipped. Of the physical distribution costs considered, the two which are geographically variable are transportation costs and pipeline inventory costs. The findings showed that for Product A, which had a value of $2,090 per unit, the geographically variable costs ranged from 76 to 56 percent of total physical distribution costs to the blocks, while Product B, which had a value of $255.20 per unit, ranged from 60 to 51 percent. It is important to note that in this study these two geographically variable costs (transportation and pipeline inventory costs) always represented *more than half* of the total costs of physical distribution. Certainly for this company such costs require careful analysis and control.

DETERMINING DISTRIBUTION TERRITORIES

The second application of the control units concerned their use in determining distribution territories. Where a company maintains multiple distribution points, it is important for it to choose the distribution point which would minimize the costs of servicing a given order. Where the company studied had actually made identical shipments to a given control block it was simple to determine which distribution point provided minimum costs. However, in the vast majority of cases identical shipments had not occurred. Ideally the costs should be available for all blocks so that alternative costs of servicing demand from various distribution points can be determined. These costs were developed by simulation shipments from alternative distribution points to 99 control blocks. Of the 99 control blocks used the company had actual sales in 37 blocks. The actual motor carrier costs and pipeline inventory costs of sales in the 37 blocks were used to check the accuracy of the simulated costs developed using the control units. The simulated (motor carrier transportation) costs were constructed by using regression line analysis to determine the association between transportation costs and each product's freight classification and weight shipped in relation to the miles involved. Three hundred and forty-three regression lines were computed involving 29 freight classifications and their respective weight breaks in relation to various mileages shipped with the resulting coefficients of correlation ranging from .999 to .973. With the usefulness of linear regression in estimating motor carrier costs proven by the high coefficients of correlation, the next problem in simulating costs involved knowing the actual highway miles between the geographic control units. Because the grid control units are based on latitude and longitude measurements, the airline distances between the centers of blocks are readily computed by using a computer program developed during the research. It was further found that by sampling various ratios of airline to highway distances within a region of the country, a usable conversion factor could be obtained. However, I must point out that there was no one conversion factor that would provide a valid relationship for all areas of the country. Thus the simulated transportation costs were developed by converting the airline distances between control units to highway distances and then using the regression equations to estimate costs. A check of the simulated transportation costs to the actual costs in the 37 blocks containing sales produced an absolute average error of less than 1 percent with a range of error from a little less than 3 percent to two tenths of one percent. Use of the simulated transportation costs combined with calculating the pipeline inventory costs associated with the use of alternative shipping points provides the total geographically variable cost patterns incurred in using alternative shipping points to the various control blocks. The delineation of distribution territories is thus derived by identifying the two adjacent control blocks whose minimum geographically variable costs favor different shipping points.

OTHER APPLICATIONS

Two other applications of the spherical control units which I will only mention briefly are their use in establishing sales territories and in location analysis. Since the control units are based solely on geographic considerations, they allow management to delineate a sales territory on marketing considerations without the necessity of using political or civil boundaries. By knowing the exact types of products and customers involved as well as the quantity and timing of sales, management can agglomerate the control units in any configuration necessary to delineate an area possessing the marketing qualities desired in the sales territories.

Finally the control units and their information concerning shipments provide an ideal modified Cartesian coordinate system for computing the various ton-mile, time-cost-ton mile, and other centers useful in determining first approximations for the location of distribution points.

SUMMARY

In conclusion it appears that a geographic marketing information system can provide an extremely useful tool for the analysis and control of various marketing activities.. Whether the system presented or some other system is used, it would appear that the subject is worthy of further research.

18. THE ROLE OF THE MARKETING EXECUTIVE IN PHYSICAL DISTRIBUTION*

Donald J. Bowersox

Seeking streamlined procedures to relieve the "profit squeeze," enterprising businessmen have become increasingly aware that physical distribution efficiency must be achieved to maintain profitable sales activity in competitive markets. When one evaluates the fact that typical profit margins represent from 1 to 10 percent of gross sales, the impact of physical distribution upon a firm's survival becomes staggering. For the average firm, physical distribution consumes between 25 and 33 percent of each sales dollar. A firm's longevity may very well depend upon reducing this third highest cost of doing business. The fundamental need to control distribution cost has resulted in widespread concentration of corporate activity upon research and implementation of scientific distribution planning.

Among the many problems consuming the time and talents of marketing executives, those most neglected relate to physical distribution. Executives, primarily concerned with developing a corporate market orientation, have rightfully concentrated attention upon molding market research, product development, pricing, personal selling, and advertising into a goal-directed marketing strategy. Experiences of firms rallying to the challenges contained in developing streamlined physical distribution systems have revealed considerable confusion concerning the proper role which the marketing department should play in meeting this crisis. There will be variations due to types of firm, industry, and most of all due to available personnel. However, to a large degree, an answer may be found by examining some factors involved in physical distribution planning.

PHYSICAL DISTRIBUTION PLANNING—A NECESSARY CORPORATE FUNCTION

Physical distribution planning may be defined as that area of business management responsible for developing systems capable of moving raw materials and finished products in a manner designed to maximize corporate marketing effort. Similar to market planning, physical distribution planning, when properly exercised, cuts across and embodies elements of most corporate decision-making centers.

Fundamental to sound distribution planning is a basic recognition that logistics represents considerably more than a facilitating function secondary to sales and marketing. The most devoted exponent of this

---

*From *Effective Marketing Coordination,* American Marketing Association, June, 1961, pp. 393–99.

viewpoint is the marketing manager who has implemented a new product promotion only to arrive at market introduction with retailers and whole-salers lacking initial stocks. Regardless of this fundamental need for split-second coordination between demand creation and physical fulfillment, marketing literature continues to describe product storage and transpor-tation—two of the many physical distribution functions—as supporting activities only worthy of cursory consideration. This historical bias in marketing thought has resulted in considerable criticism of distribution efficiency with little appreciation or positive consideration of the broader spectrum in which logistics plays a vital role.

The fundamental need for goal-directed distribution planning is clearly emphasized by the cost-service struggle currently plaguing management. It has become apparent during the last decade that profitable marketing activity can only be realized when a balance is achieved between minimum-cost distribution and the tendency to be victimized by the service spiral.

A minimum-cost distribution system is designed to move goods in the cheapest manner with little or no consideration given to the influence of service elasticity of demand. It is an economic fact that minimum-cost arangements do not necessarily represent profit maximization positions. Therefore, in distribution planning, it is necessary to safeguard against arbitrary reductions in field inventories, warehousing, and other distribu-tion components. Programs which have as their objectives short-run economies may simultaneously jeopardize market entrenchment.

Equally disadvantageous in terms of profitability is the more universal tendency among firms to maintain inventories in each customer's back-yard. Maintaining large numbers of localized field inventories is an ex-pensive habit which, in final analysis, may result in substantial losses. Variable product line turnover tends to strain service oriented distribution systems. For a typical warehouse it takes approximately 75 percent more inventory to satisfy 95 percent of customer sales from stock than it does to satisfy 80 percent. Many firms who attempt to supply in excess of 90 percent of sales from forward inventories actually lose money on many slow-moving products. Unproductive sales, from a fully allocated cost-revenue perspective, may be required to maintain line continuity. How-ever such marketing activity must be subject to stringent control.

Very few sales managers, who, by nature of their basic responsibility are inherently dedicated to high customer service levels, can adequately evaluate the impact of service upon sales. The evaluation of service as a nonprice form of competition represents one of the most complex prob-lems encountered in business planning. In its basic context the problem is simply stated as the requirement to quantify service elasticity of demand. To date, the few naive attempts to measure service-revenue relationships raise considerable doubt concerning the need for instan-taneous customer service in a wide range of industries. Evidence indicates that the critical factor in meeting customers' "real" needs may very well require consistent rather than instantaneous service. Consistent service provides the certainty required to obtain high levels of coordination between the many segmental decision centers involved in marketing.

STRATEGY IN PHYSICAL DISTRIBUTION PLANNING

Fundamental to all planning is the range of alternative strategies available. Two basic strategies are available to guide distribution planning. First, a network of distribution warehouses can be established, based upon the strategy that corporate marketing goals are best complemented by maintaining field inventories at select locations. Second, a direct distribution system may be developed based upon the strategy that risks experienced in obtaining goals are minimized by holding centralized inventories. The specific alternative justified in a given situation depends upon a wide range of marketing and distribution factors peculiar to the specific firm. For a great number of firms an effective program will be one containing a blend of these two strategies.

A discussion of the salient elements leading to a specific distribution program is obviously beyond the scope of this brief treatment. However, apparent in a close examination of basic considerations underlying alternative strategies is the fact that the marketing goals aspired to by the firm are the fundamental variables determining the configuration of a sound distribution system. It is important to fully realize that physical distribution strategy in reality means inventory strategy. It centers around the question of when to hold what and in what quantities. The only sound answer to these questions must stem from a penetrating evaluation of market intelligence and resultant marketing goals. The marketing executive represents the logical candidate for outlining broad distribution strategies since he has prime responsibility for the formulation of market targets.

THE CENTRAL ROLE OF THE MARKETING EXECUTIVE
IN PHYSICAL DISTRIBUTION PLANNING

In advocating a central role for the marketing executive in distribution planning, the case rests simply upon the fundamental need for coordination in order to avoid artificial segmentation of an otherwise integrated marketing program. The evidence supporting this position is the high degree of natural exposure the marketing executive enjoys to information necessary for effective coordination. Market information plus his relative insulation from excessive cost or service bias represent the marketing executive's basic qualification for directing distribution planning. Two comments are in order prior to elaborating upon basic prerequisites the marketing executive must acquire in order to meet this challenge.

First, in advocating distribution planning under the marketing executive, a qualification is required concerning use of the term "marketing executive." The marketing executive visualized is one who directs the many functions included in managerial marketing in contrast to one who functions exclusively as a sales manager. To properly coordinate physical distribution with other corporate activities, the marketing executive must play an active role in market research, product development, pricing, sales, and promotion.

Second, a clear distinction is required between the concepts of planning and implementation. Planning is defined as the establishment of goals and the development of broad programs to guide goal attainment. Implementation is defined as the process of goal attainment. The argument is to centralize physical distribution planning under the marketing executive but not implementation. Implementation by very nature of its deep-seated specialization must remain under the operating scrutiny of traffic and distribution professionals. The typical marketing executive lacks sufficient training and experience to direct implementation. His function is to understand sufficiently implemental problems in order to be able to integrate physical distribution considerations in overall planning.

To coordinate planning, the marketing executive must develop a sensitivity to several basic physical distribution elements.

First, a full appreciation must be developed for the fundamental importance of physical distribution in corporate planning—a point emphasized throughout this discussion. It is interesting to note that one of the prime topics at current traffic meetings is the upgrading of traffic managers to meet the broad challenges of implementing distribution programs. In contrast, it is equally interesting to observe that this AMA meeting represents one of the first marketing programs to consider physical distribution planning in a positive sense.

Second, the marketing executive must become familiar with distribution costing. On a national average, transportation services account for less than 25 percent of the total cost that occurred in marketing logistics. A total cost perspective provides the analytical framework necessary for a penetrating evaluation of alternative distribution systems. It is interesting to note that astute distribution planning will often lead to higher transportation cost. However, in any distribution system the fact that total cost is the fundamental concept is simply illustrated.

One firm currently cooperating with REA's Distribution Management Consulting Service in joint research is in the process of closing a warehouse and embarking upon a direct-to-customer distribution program. The anticipated result will be shocking if evaluated only from the traditional practice of freight accounting. The total annual transportation bill of this firm to this single market will increase substantially as a result of substituting smaller more rapid shipments to customers in place of larger consolidations to the warehouse. However, total cost will be reduced over $100,000 by the elimination of all field warehouse and inventory management costs. The net result: some $100,000 saved—$100,000 more available for product development, price competition, promotional effort, or maybe even profit.

Lastly, the marketing executive must acknowledge the need for exacting research to support distribution planning. In place of crude approximations, fictitious averages, and intuitive guessing, distribution planning must be the result of effectively utilizing electronic data processing and quantitative techniques. Many advancements in this area have mushroomed under the catchall label of operations research, including a technique commonly called linear programming. While much criticism can be voiced on the relative sterility of O.R. in providing significant payoffs to date, if quantitative techniques do hold the promise of significant payoffs, it is reasonably certain they will be realized first among logistic problems. The foundations for this prediction are simple—many elements of total cost distribution are quantifiable and can be approximated by near linear relationships. Consider the relative fruits of determining the optimum number of warehouses versus measuring the effectiveness of advertising. Alternately, consider the determination of optimum inventory levels versus the measurement of consumer self-image. The point is not to belittle the many intriguing quantitative dimensions of managerial marketing. These alternative applications are compared to emphasize the need for concentrating immediate attention upon an area holding promise of distinct and significant results. It is safe to generalize that better than 90 percent of historical distribution planning lacked the benefits of system logic, mathematical structure and, in many cases, even advanced statistical analysis. The history of distribution planning represents an era of stagnant checklists and static formulas.

These various facets—recognition of physical distribution as more than a facilitating function, understanding the analytical framework of total cost analysis and recognition of the need for research—are fundamental to distribution planning. Such planning represents one of the last frontiers for combating the tide of rising cost. Planning problems are complex. Payoffs are significant. Unfortunately, no set formula or procedure exists for guiding distribution planning. Efficient and well-coordinated physical distribution can only result from considering each firm as a specialized case requiring a tailored plan.

CONCLUSION

The basic need for coordinating distribution into the overall marketing program makes the marketing executive the logical candidate for directing physical distribution planning. It is an economic fact that, with a few minor exceptions, minimum cost distribution does not lead to maximum profits. Profits are maximized at some point along the continuum between minimum-cost and maximum-service-oriented distribution systems. This is truly the gray area of distribution—the problem of planning the proper balance. Probably no executive in top echelon management is in a better position to obtain this balance than the marketing executive, who has the basic responsibility of coordinating the firm's arsenal of marketing weapons. Only when price, product development, and promotional efforts are fully coordinated with logistical planning does the firm fully enjoy integrated marketing. The challenge is to integrate physical distribution planning into the portfolio. Only when this is accomplished will the "gray area" be replaced with a goal-directed program. The question remains— will the marketing executive rise to the challenge of positive planning in this heretofore forgotten area—to which, historically, he has been perfectly willing to allocate only the most cursory attention?

19. TOP MANAGEMENT LOOKS AT PHYSICAL DISTRIBUTION*

Anthony E. Cascino

It's about time for top management to take a look—a long, hard, incisive look—at one of the most vital areas affecting profit. It's the sequence of activities which takes the product from the plant to the customer. It's the area of physical distribution. And when the top management man does take a look he is most apt to find a neglected, uncoordinated, and disorganized area, overburdened with tradition.

All too frequently, the chaos witnessed by the top management man prompts him to turn away in despair, with the futile feeling that "it has always been thus." He concludes that it is the *undeniable* "nature of the beast" which makes it totally impossible to dislodge narrow-minded physical distribution people from their long-standing tradition, lethargy, and status quo.

But I say to you that he can no longer afford the luxury of turning away. First of all, as the top management man—he is the only one who can effectuate change and start the efficiency ball rolling—no one else has the authority. Those immediately involved who are performing various functions of physical distribution are least likely to do some dispassionate introspection into their own shopworn ways of doing things. Secondly, this sorry state of affairs exists only because top management allows it to exist. In my opinion *because* the problem is primarily an organization one, the indictment for its deplorable state must be placed squarely on the doorstep of top management, and I mean the top management of *both* the carrier *and* shipper.

---

*From *Marketing and Economic Development,* American Marketing Association, September, 1965, pp. 727–39.

The same heterogeneity and confusion has been allowed to exist in other areas of business, particularly marketing. Marketing is the complete coordination and integration of all of the forces designed to motivate the customer. This is the very essence of modern marketing. Frequently, advertising is treated as an entity apart from sales; market research is purposely divorced so its personnel will not become tainted; direct mail is used spasmodically and opportunistically; and neither knows the objectives and programs of the other. All of these elements are vital members of the same family; separate one and it will die. Until management insists on unqualified discipline and coordination of all these elements, the company will not move great volumes at respectable prices and profits.

I mention marketing at this point because not only is the need for coordination in physical distribution analogous to the need for coordination in marketing—but also because these two broad functions are, within themselves, completely interrelated. Physical distribution as a function has been, and continues to be in all too many instances, a heterogeneous hodgepodge of disconnected, unrelated autonomous activities.

Generally, the so-called orthodox way is to establish a traffic department, which tends to function as an autonomous entity, frequently totally apart and ignorant of the other activities to which it is inexorably interrelated. Then, because warehousing seems to be most closely related to production, management makes the bold and unintelligent decision to hold the production people responsible for its execution. After all, what does warehousing have to do with traffic? Also, since the sales department has the responsibility for securing the order, it is quite obvious that it should administer the function of order processing. Traffic and order processing are certainly not related!

However, because it is totally impractical to accurately define the limits of each of *these* activities, as well as the other functions of physical distribution, such as transportation, scheduling, and material handling, confusion and chaos reign. Where does traffic begin and transportation end? Where does warehousing begin and order processing end? And because these limits are not definable, *nice neat vacuums come into being.* The result is that responsibility, efficiency, and economy fall between the chairs with each part pointing his finger at the other. That is the sorry state of affairs that exists in more companies than any one of us would dare admit!

Only one person in the company has the power—and he should certainly feel the urgency—to bring order out of the chaos. Top management must establish organizational intelligence by centralizing all of the functions of physical distribution under one authority.

Otherwise, one could hardly expect those who have a vested interest in warehousing or order processing to voluntarily relinquish their prerogatives to people in traffic or transportation. The disconnected hodgepodge will continue as long as the top-management man walks away from his responsibility. That there is a serious lack of complete integration among the elements involved in physical distribution must be recognized as top management's most costly error of omission.

Let me show you how ludicrous this situation can become, and how deteriorating its effect can be on the minds of people in presumably responsible positions. Some months ago, I was talking to a friend of mine, a vice president with one of the nation's leading railroads, and frankly, I was needling him about his lack of responsiveness to an idea that we had proposed which promised a major breakthrough in the services that his railroad could offer its customers. Of course, the idea had to be tested; bugs had to be ironed out; false starts had to be overcome; but, nevertheless, it had the basic promise of a major breakthrough. My friend's response was, "Look, Tony, in your company when you get a hot idea and it pays off, the management comes up with a pat on the back, a promotion, and maybe a raise. If not a raise, certainly much compliment. If the whole thing does sour, they tell you not to be discouraged, keep getting ideas and sooner or later you'll make a breakthrough. In our business, if we get an idea, it probably tends to upset a 30-year-old structure and nobody wants to hear about it. If the idea gets a chance, and it goes sour, you're in real trouble. You probably wind up getting transferred because obviously you're not doing any good where you are. It's so much easier just to be quiet and go along." I would hate to think that the executives of all railroads behave this way, and I am certain that they do not, but in this instance you must agree with me that this man was dead. He just refused to lie down. The bell had tolled and his time was up.

Now let me assure you that while I am seemingly promiscuous in my indictments, I can recognize that the neglect of decades cannot be dispelled easily or quickly. It certainly hasn't been easy in our company, and we still have a long way to go. But we are beginning to make headway. At least we know that genuine and dynamic coordination and integration of all of the physical distribution activities are an absolute must; and that even though we instituted this action almost four years ago—we are probably realizing, at best, less than 10 percent of the efficiency and economy that is rightfully ours. In our business, we ship millions of tons of raw materials each year to our customers—the fertilizer manufacturers—and we utilize every mode of transportation. The frustrating thing is that every time we try to make a breakthrough, we are beset with resistance on the part of the people whose cooperation we so desperately need.

Let me show you another instance of organized lethargy. One of our customers asked the railroads for a freight reduction—supported by ensuing economies—that would help increase the volume of his business with a corresponding increase in business for the railroads. The railroads in question refused. The manner in which they refuse is most debilitating. They set up a parade of horrors. "If we do it for you, we have to do it for thousands of others." "The ruling bodies will object." "The unions will resist." However, not to be denied, we helped this customer develop a new distribution scheme using rail, water, and truck that succeeded in reducing his distribution cost. And only this customer was able to use this system of distribution. What happened? The same railroads who previously refused this customer the rate reduction responded by cutting the rail rates to all points in this area. Unfortunately, they had already lost our customer's tonnage, which was under a five-year contract. In essence, they compounded their first error of inactivity and reduced all their rates and needlessly gave away several hundred thousand dollars each year. Their first move was inertia—their second, pointlessness.

Of course, everyone knew the motor truck was going to be a passing fancy, a gadget that would never amount to anything commercially. This was the attitude of railroads during the twenties and the thirties. Look what happened! Just about all the intercity tonnage growth in the past 20 years has been by motor carriage. The railroads thought that they were in the railroad business. It never occurred to them that they were in the transportation business, moving people and materials in concert with a growing economy. I don't want you to think that this is just my own personal opinion. Let me quote from a very wonderful book, *Innovation in Marketing*, by Dr. Ted Levitt. This is what he says about the railroads. "The railroads are in trouble today not because the need was filled by cars, trucks, and airplanes, but because it was not filled by the railroads themselves. They let others take customers away from them because they assumed themselves to be in the railroad business rather than in the transportation business . . . they were railroad-oriented instead of transportation-oriented; product-oriented instead of customer-oriented."

Another example of clinging to the past is our old friend, the boxcar. For years, the boxcar remained unchanged. Sure, it changed from wood to steel, but even this change took valuable time; it took years. The railroads failed to appreciate that they were a part of a giant nationwide material handling system. They could have developed new systems of material flow that would result in many economies for their customers and themselves. Surely their top management didn't look beyond the heavy watch chains that draped from their vests. Don't think I am anti-railroad. Our company couldn't afford to be. The same ancient, venerated thinking also applied to our own industry. *Things have a way of developing by chance and remain unchallenged for years.* For example, all raw materials suppliers use the same supply of boxcars, when they can get them. This is considered to be the acceptable way to handle materials. The industry also suffers from seasonality, shipping about 65 percent of the total volume in a two-month spring season. Again, this condition is accepted as an unalterable fact of life. During this heavy shipping season the industry is plagued by car shortages and damaged lading from poor rail equipment. Sure, we have some covered hoppers, but for years the use and deployment of these cars was not under the jurisdiction of the traffic manager. This equipment was operated from one of our mines. As a consequence, one of our hopper cars was gone for 18 months, and no one at IMC was aware of this lamentable fact. What's worse, no one even cared.

Obviously, in a highly seasonal business, costly field warehouses must be maintained to help us through the peak shipping season. These warehouses were under the jurisdiction of our production group, and their use and location was strictly a function of the overflow of their production runs. This resulted in storage of product convenient to production, but at great distances from consuming markets. In one instance, we had product in a warehouse for three years. Its final disposition could only be achieved at bargain prices.

Again, our order system depended primarily on the memories of several men in the order-processing department. Only heaven could help us if either man took sick during the peak season, and we accepted the peak as something that had always been with us and only an act of God could change. We traced and tried to expedite sales orders in freight cars moving throughout the country. All shippers do this, but the futility of trying to do this during the peak season left many of our customers disenchanted with our efforts. During the heavy selling season it has become standard practice to be completely deluged with urgent calls from hundreds of customers—night and day—saying "Where is the car?" "Can I be assured that it will be here on time?" You can just imagine a beehive of activity, long-distance phone calls, distorted information, inaccurate recording of data, and then the clincher—the delayed arrival of one car during the heavy selling season could jeopardize as much as 10 percent of our customer's annual profits. We also had the attitude that since we sold f.o.b. our plant, our responsibility ended once we were able to land and load a freight car. The red wagon was the customer's—read the contract!

Our company was in the very same state of apathy, inertia, and status quo, of chaos and muddle with which I have accused both the railroads and our own fertilizer industry. I wish I could say, at this point, that I saw the problem, rolled up my sleeves and set everything right, but such was not the case. The fact of the matter is that it was a most fortuitous circumstance which started us on the right course. I was asked by a friend of mine, Martin Gainsbrugh, to address the National Industrial Conference Board as part of a panel of four. Since each member of the panel was both opinionated and strong-minded, the Conference Board left it to the panel to assign itself each of the four subjects.

We drew straws, and I was stuck with the subject of physical distribution. Incidentally, it should be most illuminating that this was considered by all to be the least attractive area for discussion. And frankly, at that time, I knew little about the general field of physical distribution. So I asked our director of transportation, Gene Landis, to put together a comprehensive collection of basic material. Since I was shortly taking my family to Disneyland—via the railroads—I would have plenty of time to read and digest. What a shock! It was embarrassingly apparent to me that we were floundering, inefficient, and archaic.

As soon as I got back to Skokie, I called Gene. We plunged into a thorough review of our total effort—facing up to its inadequacies, its barriers, its omissions, and most important of all, its basic philosophy. Concurrent with the establishment of a complete centralization of all of the elements of physical distribution within a single area of responsibility was another most important recognition. *That is the inseparability between the acquisition of the order and its fulfillment.* As Professor Ed Smykay says in his book, *Physical Distribution Management,* "Physical distribution embodies the other half of marketing." The marketing coin (as we at IMC view it) has on one side all of the activities—coordinated into an integrated whole—which concern themselves with getting the order. These include advertising, merchandising, direct mail, the broadcast media, direct selling and several others. The other side of the coin consists of a similarly integrated whole of all the activities involved in physically providing the product. As a result, the newly created department of distribution became an integral part of the marketing division. This interrelation between selling and physical distribution is inviolate in our business, which is mainly characterized by the economics of shipping low-cost bulk commodities. The efficiency with which the order is handled is as important in securing the order as are the sales and merchandising efforts.

For example, the price of a ton of phosphate rock, f.o.b. the mine, is about $7; the costs of warehousing, freight, and handling frequently total an additional cost of $11; so that by the time the customer gets the product, his landed cost is $18. Now, if we are not aggressive, innovative, imaginative, and resourceful—and if one of our competitors is, and he discovers a way by which he can cut his distribution costs by $3—we're dead! Even if we wanted to stupidly offset our competitor's more efficient means of shipping with a reduced f.o.b. price for our product, we don't have that much profit margin to play with.

Therefore, we have no other choice but to strive for the lowest distribution costs conceivable; and we dare not let any sacred cows, tradition, inertia, and indolence impede our aspiration. With this objective indelibly imprinted on our minds, our first major step was to remove all barriers by establishing a distribution department with complete responsibility for traffic, transportation facilities, warehousing, order processing, shipment scheduling, and material handling. Our newly organized ocean freighting offices in New York, Vancouver, and Tampa were also placed in the distribution department.

The first prerequisite had been met and we had organization working for us, not against us. With complete and centralized responsibility, we had eliminated the vacuums, the space between the chairs into which important details could fall. We had the right people and the proper disciplines; we were ready to move. So while we may have been late in acting, you must give us some "Brownie points" for moving fast once we had been exposed to the opportunity.

The first order of business was to tackle the problem of car shortage. We went out and leased 1,500 freight cars. In order to give you the proper perspective of this bold step, our next closest competitor has a fleet of less than 100 cars. But our greatly increased fleet made the function of supervision and control most critical. We had to know the whereabouts of the equipment to economically and effectively use these cars as sales tools. Our distribution men and our data processing department jointly outlined a computer car location system to some 30 railroads. The railroad computers transmit to us daily some 6,000 car reportings. Each morning we know not only the whereabouts of our own leased equipment but every one of our shipments on the railroads in our system. TELS-CAR is the name we have given this car control system. TELS-CAR enables us to inform our customers of the exact location of his shipment. He doesn't have to trace his car and neither do we. The computers, the railroads' and ours, do the job far more effectively. This frees both the railroad men and our own men for more productive work and relieves the customer's mind from the worry that a single car, lost or delayed during a critical time, could cost him 10 percent of his yearly profits. With this much at stake, you can imagine our customer's concern for each car carrying valuable raw materials to him. TELS-CAR provides us with those essential elements of information which enable us to virtually guarantee on-time delivery of each and every car.

But TELS-CAR represents something much bigger at IMC. It is representative of our innovative spirit, which is the cornerstone of our whole corporate philosophy. We harbor no sacred cows. No matter how successful we may have been yesterday, today everything is subject to review and scrutiny, in a constant pursuit for new and better ways. In this instance, we needed a better way, and we also found a way to make profitable use of our computers between midnight and 5 A.M. We found a better way to serve our customers, and in serving them, we completely changed the relationships we had with some 30 railroads. Again, the idea was resisted with misgivings, skepticism, and inertia, but at no time were we doubtful that ultimate success would be ours.

Actually our car control system is a by-product of our new order processing system which is not fully automated. A customer order can now be fully processed and the customer given his car number, date of shipment, and weight as quickly as one hour after the receipt of his order. Sales and market analysis statistics become readily available because all orders are in the computer. It is only a matter of punching the right buttons on the computer to receive whatever information may be required. As residual benefits, the new system cuts human errors to a minimum and reduces the cost of processing a customer's order.

The principle of bringing all of our talents, disciplines, and professionalists face-to-face with our customers is standard practice throughout the company. This has made IMC known in depth. The majority of our customers is called upon by not only the salesman, but a dozen or more IMC specialists including agronomists, accountants, scientists, technicians, and representatives of the physical distribution department. The channels of communication have been opened and this very day, I'm sure that at least 30 customers have spoken directly and on a first-name basis with our distribution staff.

In turn, our distribution people have effectively moved some 12,000,000 tons of materials to customers all over the world. They have established new materials handling procedures, using tote-bins and pneumatic cars. So effectively have they used TELS-CAR with our leased fleet that the first year of the fleet's existence, they moved the cars over 20,000,000 miles. Bear in mind that this was the performance for the first year and that was only 10 percent short of the break-even point. These examples point clearly to our strong philosophy of customer service. We will use any resource we possess on behalf of customer's benefit and progress.

On their periodic calls on customers, our distribution men found that many of our accounts were not aware of important developments in transportation, packaging, and materials handling. To fill this vacuum of knowledge, we initiated and now publish *The Transportation Newsletter,* which is sent to some 3,000 customers. It is written specifically for our customers, and we know they eagerly anticipate each issue. Some time back, we conducted a survey among our customers to see if they thought the newsletter was really worthwhile. Unless it was endorsed by a majority, we would kill it! Our customers protested "Don't you dare discontinue the *Transportation Newsletter.* It's the single most valuable publication from IMC." To my knowledge, we are the only company giving this particular customer service.

Furthermore, to develop a close relation with marketing, we have our distribution men take an active part in our sales meetings. It is important for our salesmen to know the fundamentals of effective physical distribution. Our distribution men are part of a marketing team which is also responsible for staging customer meetings. Case in point, our Great Train meeting last year. We decided to run a customer meeting on board a passenger train. Our marketing heads outlined the physical requirements to several members of the distribution department, who in turn arranged with the Milwaukee Railroad to supply a train. The requirements were such that there were a great many doubts as to whether such a train meeting was possible. But it was possible! A dining car was converted into a small theatre for 50 customers. Films and slides were projected; stereo sound filled the car; speakers, including a distribution man, gave forth; and in all, we had the most unusual program ever delivered aboard a moving train. This is the type of innovation that we demand of our distribution group, because we feel that this group must be a part of our total marketing effort.

Our company constantly strives to help our customers help themselves. We do this through a total service marketing program which includes management seminars for the heads of our customer companies, training of customer sales and production personnel, customer advisory panels, and a host of other activities. We write books and pamphlets designed to assist our customers with their problems. Our distribution people participate in these activities as speakers and writers. In our book, *Managing for Profit*, which covers the management and marketing aspects of the fertilizer business, there is a chapter devoted to distribution written by one of our distribution men. We also have a booklet titled *Saving Transportation Dollars*, which was also written by the distribution group.

It may seem a little unusual to talk of a railroad car as a merchandising tool, but that's exactly what our Sparger Car is, a valuable merchandising tool. Designed specifically for our industrial chemicals department, the Sparger Car has a capacity of 100 tons. The advantage to our customer is that this car can be unloaded in only one third the time required by standard methods. The dry bulk chemical is mixed with water and pumped into storage tanks at the customer's plant. The chemicals we ship in this car are more easily transported in a dry form, but the customer can use the material only as a liquid. The Sparger Car gives us the opportunity to ship dry and deliver wet—advantages for both buyer and seller.

The future holds promise of new innovations in physical distribution. Many benefits would be ours if we were able to transport our products by pipeline. But why not consider the railroads which have a valuable tool at their fingertips—the integral train. Properly implemented, more product could be moved in less time at a cost comparable with that of a pipeline. We have already experimented with the integral train idea and we've found that this is only half of the concept. Take an integral train, combine it with a backhaul arrangement, and whole new market areas open up to you. As a matter of fact, you can actually *manufacture* new markets! Gentlemen, we've already broken the barriers and have disposed of over 300,000 tons a year at a point where no new market previously existed.

With our seasonalized demands for products we have seasonalized requirements for warehousing. When we need a warehouse, we build a portable one by blowing up a "portable air structure." We are planning one now for a location near Minneapolis, Minnesota. It will be the largest of its kind with a capacity of 55,000 tons. Next year, or the year after, this warehouse may be in Kansas, or Ohio. New, larger air structure warehouses may be located anywhere from coast to coast. This puts an adequate supply of product at the doorsteps of our customers, wherever they are.

I mentioned earlier that our own industry was shackled by tradition, the tradition of selling and shipping 65 percent of our total production in only two months of the year. There are obvious problems which result from this kind of situation; inefficient usage of plant facilities, warehouses, railroad cars, trucks, and many others. But in spite of the fact that this situation had always existed, it became clear that sooner or later someone would change it. That someone would then have a great advantage in that he would be able to impose on the marketplace those changes which would suit him best. Those remaining would then be forced to subscribe to the new rules, whether they liked them or not.

We decided that we would rather be the innovator. Again we sacrificed the sacred cow, and dared to change the parameters which describe our industry. Today our customers are accepting delivery of materials in the so-called off-season. It costs them less to warehouse than it costs us, and these savings are passed along to our customers. With material on hand, they can begin their annual production runs earlier in the season, avoiding the last-minute stampede to meet orders. Deseasonalization has had a tremendous effect on physical distribution. It results in more efficient use of our leased fleet of 1,500 cars, as well as the additional 4,500 railroad-owned cars we use in the peak of the season.

I cannot, at this time, go into the details of other breakthroughs we've made in physical distribution as the result of deseasonalization. Many are in the planning and experimental stages and it would be inappropriate to discuss them now. But you can be assured that we are challenging every minute facet of our procedures to see if they can be made to yield to a better way.

I don't want to belabor the point, but to fully appreciate the potential we have, you must realize that we hold nothing to be sacred, everything is subject to scrutiny and review—including the physical distribution of our salesmen. Ask yourself, "How does the salesman get from one customer to another?" By car, of course. But is a car the best way? Certainly! Isn't it? Today our salesmen are calling on our customers in Greenbriar Mobile Sales Offices. Since the salesman has to have some kind of vehicle anyway, why not make that vehicle more than just a means of transportation? Why not provide the salesman with all the tools he needs to make an effective sales presentation? The Greenbriars are offices on wheels, heated or air-conditioned as the weather requires. They're stocked with literature, flip-charts, product displays, even a sound slide-film projector and screen. Once the sale is made, the salesman has the necessary tools at his fingertips to make some simple soil tests. The Greenbriars are certainly much more efficient than the conventional sedan. They represent a break with tradition. At our company, tradition is only as good as the results. If something else turns out to be better than Greenbriars, the Greenbriars will be replaced.

Gentlemen, if time permitted, I could give you an endless list of accomplishments; about our unique use of backhaul arrangements in every mode of transportation; about our use of company planes to move not only our own people, but our customers; about our ocean freighting subsidiaries at our major points of export; about how we found ourselves in the ship agency and chartering business; about how our distribution men work with customers all over the world, bringing the benefits heretofore confined to the United States to our many customers overseas, as we expand our operations to cover the globe. But time doesn't permit me to illustrate why I feel certain that we are realizing merely 10 percent of the economies and benefits which can be ours, and that we still have a long way to go.

I began this talk by seriously doubting that top management has given physical distribution full recognition of the opportunity that lies in most corporations for cost and service efficiencies. Examples of failures to optimize physical distribution concepts were given about railroads and industry, particularly my own industry. But I think I have also demonstrated that once a top manager sees the light, things can and do happen. It is most important that top management understand the principles of physical distribution, that the total system concept be made clear to them, and that top management remove the barriers that always exist in large and small corporations. To reap all the benefits and blessings that flow from well-integrated physical movements systems, responsibility and the corresponding authority must be given to the distribution member of the organization. Otherwise, new titles and a paint job will only color the exterior, and the internal mechanisms will continue to clash and miss as always. Innovations must be introduced in a business climate that will permit even the smallest idea to grow into new and rewarding concepts.

Suggested additional AMA readings

Anderson, Henry. "Problems Peculiar to Export Sales Forecasting," *Journal of Marketing*, April, 1960, pp. 39–42.

Barton, Samuel G. "A Marketing Model for Short-Term Prediction of Consumer Sales," *Journal of Marketing*, July, 1965, pp. 19–29.

Brown, D. A.; Buck, S. F.; and Pyatt, F. G. "Improving the Sales Forecast for Consumer Durables," *Journal of Marketing Research*, August, 1965, pp. 229–35.

Brown, Rodger A. "Forecasting Methods of Operation," in *Dynamic Marketing in a Changing World*, pp. 290–94. Chicago: American Marketing Association, 1960.

Brye, Stanley. "Why Kill the Passenger Train?" *Journal of Marketing*, January, 1964, pp. 1–6.

Constantin, James A., "The Use of Transportation Data in Market Pattern Analysis," *Journal of Marketing*, July, 1964, pp. 74–78.

Dahlberg, Arthur O. "Economic Forecasting and the Consultant," *New Directions in Marketing*, pp. 173–84. Chicago: American Marketing Association, 1965.

Dean, Joel. "Competitive Pricing in Railroad Freight Rates," *Journal of Marketing*, April, 1961, pp. 22–27.

Farmer, Richard N. "Marketing the Transportation System," *Journal of Marketing*, January, 1964, pp. 54–57.

Fernald, Robert O. "Three Ways to Make an Industrial Forecast," in *Marketings' Role in Scientific Management*, pp. 381–400. Chicago: American Marketing Association, 1957.

Foulke, J. Brian. "How to Do Short Range Sales Forecasting," in *Effective Marketing Coordination*, pp. 209–215. Chicago: American Marketing Association, 1961.

Haring, Albert. "Establishing the Market Index for Your Company," *Advancing Marketing Efficiency*, pp. 417–20. Chicago: American Marketing Association, 1958.

Johnson, Robert W. "Forecasting in a Basic Materials Company," in *Dynamic Marketing for a Changing World*, pp. 279–89. Chicago: American Marketing Association, 1960.

Kelley, Eugene; Lazo, Hector; Corbin, Arnold; and Kahn, Edward. *Marketing Management: An Annotated Bibliography*. Chicago: American Marketing Association, 1963.

Kramer, Walter. "How Marketing Research Can Help Railroads," *Journal of Marketing*, October, 1961, pp. 39–46.

Lasher, E. C. R. "Logistics Support in Distribution for Effective Market Programming," *Marketing Precision and Executive Action*, pp. 463–66. Chicago: American Marketing Association, 1962.

McLaughlin, Robert L. "The Breakthrough in Sales Forecasting," *Journal of Marketing*, April, 1963, pp. 46–54.

Parkany, John. "A New Approach to Sales Forecasting and Production Scheduling," *Journal of Marketing*, January, 1961, pp. 14–21.

Roberts, Harry V. "A Technique for Appraising and Improving Forecasts," in *The Broadening Perspective of Marketing*, pp. 97–102. Chicago: American Marketing Association, 1956.

Semon, Thomas T. "A Simple Seasonal Pattern," *Journal of Marketing*, July, 1958, pp. 62–63.

Vreeland, Carl. "The Jantzer Method of Short-Range Forecasting," *Journal of Marketing*, April, 1963, pp. 66–69.